For a Handful
of Feathers

For a Handful
of Feathers

Guy de la Valdéne

THE ATLANTIC MONTHLY PRESS
NEW YORK

Published simultaneously in Canada
Printed in the United States of America

FIRST EDITION

Library of Congress Cataloging-in-Publication Data

De la Valdéne, Guy.
  For a handful of feathers / Guy de la Valdéne.—1st ed.
  ISBN 0-87113-618-X
  1. Quail culture—Florida—Gadsden County. 2. Bobwhite—Florida—
Gadsden County. 3. Game farms—Florida—Gadsden County.
I. Title.
SF510.Q2D4   1995   636.6'3—dc20   95-11907

DESIGN BY LAURA HAMMOND HOUGH

The Atlantic Monthly Press
841 Broadway
New York, NY 10003

10 9 8 7 6 5 4 3 2 1

To Clippy
with love

And you will go where the crows go
and you will know what crows know

After you have learned all their secrets
and think the way they do and your love
caresses their feathers like the walls of a midnight clock,
they will fly away and take you with them.

And you will go where the crows go
and you will know what crows know.

—Richard Brautigan, from "Crow Maiden"

Hunting with a Friend

by Jim Harrison

I've begun to believe that some of us are not as evolved as we may think. Up in the country, in my prolonged childhood, I liked best to walk, fish, and hunt where there were few, if any, people. After a ten-year hiatus for college and trying to be Rimbaud, Dostoevsky, and James Joyce, not to speak of William Faulkner, in New York, Boston, and San Francisco, I found myself back in northern Michigan walking, fishing, and hunting. There are a lot more people now, but there are still plenty of places where they aren't. Tennis, golf, and drugs didn't work for me, so for the past thirty years my abiding passions are still centered on upland game birds, fish, and idling around fields, mountains, and the woods on foot, studying habitat, but mostly wandering and looking things over.

On the surface, and maybe underneath, this may be regarded by some as an idiot's life. In the very long struggle to find out your own true character there is the real possibility you'll discover a simpleton beneath the skin, or at least something deeply peculiar. But then you slowly arrive at a point where you accept your comfortable idiosyncrasies, aided in part by a study of your sporting friends, who are capable of no less strange behavior. A few years back I tried to explain to a long table of studio executives the pleasures of walking around wild country in the moonlight. They nodded evasively, but I could tell they thought I was daft. The same tale told to two or three of my favorite hunting or fishing companions would be received as utterly ordinary, say on the level of drinking too much good wine. It's simply the kind of thing you do when your curiosity arouses you.

In *For a Handful of Feathers* Guy de la Valdéne has written a splendid and compelling book about quail. There is a great body of information I didn't know about in the book and certainly had no idea he knew about. It occurred to me after reading it that one reason you stick with a friend is because they are able to surprise and enliven you. In some respects *For a Handful of Feathers* is a nineteenth-century rather than twentieth-century book; in it you will find none of the shrill gunslinging, the otiose "how to do it to get the most out of it" attitudes of the contemporary hunting mainstream, an arena that has become so mechanized that you may as well stay home and fiddle with the Internet for all the good it does your soul. But herein we have an exhaustive sporting coda that doesn't presume that we hunt in a vacuum, as if we could separate the land from the creatures that live there. The death of hunting will come not from the largely imagined forces of anti-hunting but by the death of habitat, the continuing disregard for the land in the manner of a psychopath burning down a house and then wondering why he still can't live there. This illusion of separateness is maddening. We are nature, too, surely as a chimp or trout.

I first met Guy de la Valdéne back in the late sixties through my friend Tom McGuane. McGuane was living in the Florida Keys and I had come down from Michigan to explore the fishing, which we attempted to do on the severest budget with his old Roberts skiff and a malfunctioning twenty-horse outboard, none of which vitiated the pleasure of our first trips out on the flats. At the Sea Center, a hangout for the saltwater guides, we met this oddly formal Frenchman, Guy de la Valdéne, who was in the middle of a sixty-day booking with Woody Sexton, the pre-eminent Keys guide of the time. We thought this a little strange, not to say expensive, though later it occurred to me that after this first learning foray Valdéne was able to buy a skiff and guide himself.

The next spring the four of us, including Russell Chatham, fished in tandem for thirty days, and we have continued to do so for years, barring occasional absences for poverty, mental problems, divorce. McGuane threw in the towel first, recognizing the attritional factors of Key West before the rest of us were ready to, for all the various reasons of foolhardiness. Key West before its gradual and inevitable gentrification was a nexus, particularly in the seventies, for crazed and random hormones, free-flowing alcohol and pharmaceuticals, the kind of behavioral skew that requires some time to effect recovery, a euphemism for cold sweat and prayer. But the fishing was wonderful.

After that first full spring of fishing in 1970 Guy came

to northern Michigan to hunt woodcock and grouse with me, and he has done so ever since, missing only two years out of twenty-five. The first time out seemed a little awkward, with Valdéne appearing in European hunting clothes, but he allayed the suspicions of two of my local friends by bagging fifteen of the sixteen birds he shot at, filling out the limits for the rest of us, who got only one or two. When you are younger you waste a great deal of time figuring out whether you are good or not. Later on you *know* perfectly well, good or bad or indifferent, and the problem drifts away. Valdéne is the best shot, and also the best saltwater fly caster I know, but I should add that this apparently isn't very important to him. It may have been once, but it hasn't been for a long time. He tends to think of such discussions as tasteless or impolite. When you both shoot at a particular bird at once he invariably says, "your bird." This would get irritating if it weren't sincere, though it is a decided improvement over those who claim every bird.

In the ensuing years we made a number of trips, including early ones when I was still a work journalist and Guy a photographer: the southern coast of Ecuador, where we first fished billfish on flies in the early seventies and Guy took the first underwater photos of fighting billfish (a bit perilous); and his home area of Normandy, where we followed a stag hunt. Later came Costa Rican fishing, but we mostly stayed in the states, fishing in the Florida Keys, fishing and hunting in Montana, and trading visits to our own locales for grouse and woodcock in Michigan and quail in north Florida.

Strangely, as you grow older, if you can't hunt with any of two or three friends you'd rather hunt alone. Newcomers make the grievous error of talking to your dogs, which are confused by such breaches in taste, or they whine about the weather. Admittedly there are the odd miseries of the season, such as when one hunts on days where normally the idea of a mere short walk would be repellent. Once, in the Upper Peninsula, it began to snow so hard in the middle of a woodcock flight that we couldn't see each other more than ten feet away, but my bitch Tess continued to point. Valdéne laughed at each flush while I began to brood about finding the car. He had on rubber boots and I didn't, so he offered to carry me across a wide slough with at least a foot of water. He's rather sturdy and didn't seem to mind my two hundred pounds (a bit upwards of that), so we set off toward the car with me holding on like a papoose. It was even funny when we pitched forward, with at least the floundering and splashing getting the dog's attention off the birds. She was very young then and you don't want to call a young dog off active scent even if it means freezing to death. Afterwards, it was one of those rare occasions when a glass of whiskey actually tasted delicious.

Most of our hunting days are relatively wordless, a testament to the quality of attention the sport requires, the absolute absorption in the day itself. By midafternoon, however, the limited talk tends to direct itself toward what we're going to cook for dinner. Since Guy is French and my tastes run in that direction too, we never settle for something simple. A couple of hours of cooking relieves the bone weariness rather than adding to it. In hundreds of meals we try to avoid repetition, so the imagination is fully engaged, even during the onerous chore of plucking birds (it is a sin against God to skin them). Another boon is that we are able, during bird season, despite up to six hours of walking a day, to gain weight. This cannot be humanly accomplished without night after night of eating multiple courses of quail, wild piglet, venison, mallards, sweetbreads, grouse, woodcock, lobsters, oysters, and crab. Out of respect for my gout we rarely eat beef during bird season. Over the years Guy has nobly and politely tried to adjust to American wines but prefers French, which is now about all we drink, even if it is simple Côtes de Rhone, though there are quirky sideroads into Tuscany and Australia.

Ultimately, *For a Handful of Feathers* is a portrait of a hunter and reminiscent of Turgenev's *A Sportsman's Sketches*. It is the effort of one man to completely understand the section of land on which he lives. Nothing is left out that should be there. Hunting can be a good experience for your soul, to the degree that you refuse to exclude none of the realities of the natural world, including a meditation on why you hunt, perhaps an ultimately unanswerable question. I have often thought the urge to hunt to be genetic rather than manly or heroic, whatever those characteristics mean in a world where the word *honor* itself is a joke. Unlike our forefathers or Native Americans we don't have to do it, but then I suspect they also hunted when they didn't have to, for the sheer joy of it. *For a Handful of Feathers* addresses these questions, but more so, it concerns itself with how we use our land, what we can and can't do for the creature life upon it. There's an old saw, certainly politically incorrect but a specific tonic in a bleak and weary age: "The predator husbands its prey."

No bird soars too high,
if he soars with his own wings.
—William Blake

Prologue

I live on the outskirts of Tallahassee, Florida, on a farm in Gadsden County, eleven miles west of Coon Bottom and thirteen miles south of Booger Bay, Georgia. The region is referred to as the red hills of Florida for its abundance of clay and the rolling nature of its topography. All in all, a fine place to live, particularly if one has the means to travel every so often to a place where people speak the King's English and where chewing tobacco is thought of in the same vein as messing one's pants. A small price to pay, I might add, for an otherwise wild and as yet untainted piece of geography.

Shade-tobacco farming in Gadsden County (specifically, cultivation of the broad outer leaf used to wrap Cuban cigars) had enriched the local economy since the turn of the century. Until 1960 or so, the sweet fragrance of tobacco was carried on every breeze, coins jingled in men's pockets, and life in the county was sweet and full of promise. However, as with most undertakings that rely on the poverty of one class for the benefit of another, there are always tiers of hungrier people with lower expectations who will work for less. This is how Gadsden County lost its hold on the tobacco market to the field hands of Central America.

A handful of long, rectangular barns, fashioned out of the hearts of tall slash pines, once swollen with stringers of curing tobacco leaves and the smoke from carefully tended charcoal fires, stand as silent witnesses. Resin lingers in the darkness of the few remaining barns, but outside the wood shingles are weather-warped and the roofs dull. They endure, unused except as occasional hideouts for children and as shelters for the mice and swallows that come and go through the wind tears of summer storms.

The county's sudden loss of wealth (Gadsden was, for a moment in history, the richest county in the state) left a huge workforce wanting and unemployed, an undertow of penurious souls that never recovered economically. Thirty years later, at the end of every month, mothers send their children to public school on empty stomachs. Food swells the grocery shelves, but in many households the money has run out. I live in the poorest county in Florida.

My land lies between the sandy coastal soil south of Tallahassee and the flat piney forests of Georgia. The barrel-like clay hills, hardwood bottoms, and deep chasms that cut into the earth exist, I am told, because this is where the south-ern grade of the Appalachian mountain range falls to the sea, a romantic theory that explains some of the tortured gullies in which my turkeys strut.

This earth is not as rich as the tenderloin of grade-one soil that runs north and south between Thomasville, Georgia, and Tallahassee, Florida, but then, neither am I, so my aim is to improve what I have as best I can within certain financial boundaries.

The farm was once part of a much larger plantation and, throughout its existence, has produced cotton and the slaves to pick it, cattle, shade tobacco, peanuts, corn, and a large, rambunctious Southern family. In 1990 I bought eight hundred acres of what remained of the homestead, changed its name and status to Dogwood Farm, and to the utter delight of my hunting dogs—Robin, the English springer spaniel who looks like a Stubbs painting; Mabel, the doltish lemon-and-white English pointer; and Carnac, the roan-colored French Brittany puppy who resembles a suckling pig—pro-ceeded to grow birds: wild eastern bobwhite quail (*Colinus virginianus* for those interested in the specifics of what things are and where they come from).

The woods, which comprise 50 percent of the prop-erty, are composed of second-growth loblollies, slash, a hand-ful of long-leaf pine trees, thousands of white, red, and water oaks, gum trees, hickories, dogwoods, ironwoods, chinaber-ries, pecans, poplars, willows, sassafras, magnolias, and crab apples. A number of eighty-year-old live oaks round out the selection. Uniformity bores me senseless, and while some of the finest plantations north and east of me grow beautiful, manicured rows of plum-perfect pinewoods, no matter how straight and how old those trees may be (and I can attest that they are), a few hours under their homogeneous canopy make me long for the garish play of light that glances over the boughs of my hardwoods.

Our most eccentric tree, the live oak (*Quercus virginiana*), also named after the state of Virginia, spends its life draped in Spanish moss, a rootless epiphyte that the Southeast Indian women fashioned into skirts and which African slaves later used to stuff their mattresses. These are hugely reassuring trees, trees that define insouciance, poets among trees, and I feel a kinship to them, as I would feel a kinship to baobabs if I lived in Senegal. As luck would have it, bobwhite quail relish the bittersweet taste of acorns, and in plentiful years— about one out of every three—they march down to the bottoms, to where the hardwoods grow thick, where the deer and the turkey live, and where food falls from the sky.

The other half of the farm is given over to half a dozen fields and abandoned pastures. One such cornfield was so large—two hundred acres—that I didn't know how to manage it until it was brought to my attention that quail, like most gallinaceous birds, are stalkers of edges. Because small openings yield more edges than larger ones, I broke this monotonous expanse into ten or twelve long, narrow fields with trees, food plots, and cover. The pastures yield Pensacola Bahia grass and to a lesser degree Bermuda grass, thick, mat types, savored by cows and by bobwhites during their nesting season, grasses that once established are difficult to get rid of. Two small wet-weather ponds stain both ends of the two-hundred-acre field, and a thirty-acre lake, teeming with brim and black bass, fills an old hardwood bottom. On the edge of this lake I built a cabin, officially a writing studio, but in reality the quarters I escape to as early as possible each day and inside of which I spy through high-powered binoculars on wood ducks and ospreys, martins, bluebirds, the quail and doves that visit my feeder, otters, snakes, and whatever other creatures nature pushes across my lenses.

In the South, a bird means a quail; a mess of birds, a bunch of quail; and a bird dog, a quail dog. To confuse the issue slightly, in some regions, while black bass are thought of as trout, bobwhites are referred to as partridge. However, regardless of colloquial designation, the history of the bobwhite quail is also the history of the men and women who shaped this continent, a broad spectrum of social, historical, and economic personalities, from the Creek Indians who snared quail to the market hunters who netted them, the sharecroppers who ground-sluiced them, the farmers, doctors, and schoolteachers who hunted up and down miles of multiflora fence rows, flushed bobwhites across bean fields, and killed them on the edge of the broom sedge, to the Yankees who, to this day, wear fancy clothes and chase after quail sitting high in the saddle of expensive gaited horses.

A covey of quail is a coterie, an assembly of coquettes and dandies. Eight to ten inches tall, ovate in shape, balanced on overly long toes, scaly legs, and fat thighs, they assume an impeccably upright posture, particularly when perched on logs and fence posts. These are birds that display a vocabulary of fall colors with lively black eyes and strong, horny beaks designed to deal with stubborn seeds. But in hand they feel like soft-boiled eggs, brown, buff, ash, black, and chestnut-colored eggs whose barred and crescent patterns remind one of swollen leaves on the bottom of a pond. Bobwhite quail are plump and malleable like cotton candy. Tender birds without the musculature of distant travelers or even roamers, quail gravitate to where the food is plentiful and within walking distance; they enjoy both grit and chatter and are loath to fly for any reason. The male bird wears a white mask over his cheeks and chin and black eye stripes down to his beak. The female's coloring matches her mate's—a similarity of plumage usually indicates an inclination to sharing of parental duties—except that the hen's mask is ochre yellow in coloring. The entire covey faces its destiny with poised terror.

The fact that I devote a certain effort to the well-being of bobwhites during these times of political perjury, fast food, and baboonlike talk shows falls on understanding ears in this part of the country; ears that have been conditioned to the hubristic sounds of spring whistling, the startled scatterings of roadside coveys, the resonance of autumn guns, and the invigorating cracklings of fried quail and okra. So when I am asked what kind of a farm I own I say, "A bird farm," readily admitting to being, by modern criteria, a bum. However, instead of being questioned about my motives or the rationale behind them, I am queried on the condition of the land, the dogs, and that year's crop of quail. The questions entertain well-hidden remembrances, reminders of gentler days when slow dancing, drive-in movies, spandex girdles, and Golden Hawk Studebakers were fashionable.

When I am asked the same question up north, I reply, "A big farm."

"Oh! You mean an everything farm?" he or she asks, backpedaling for all it's worth in an effort to forestall any thought I may have regarding honking on about rural life, mud holes, and chiggers.

"Yeah," I answer, looking the asker in the eye. And much to everyone's relief, that's usually the end of it.

For reasons of life, death, and changing interests, the farm had not been managed for quail for fifteen years prior to my arrival. Deer were culled from tree stands and doves were shot in the cornfields, but for a long time there was only one serious quail hunter: a fine old Southern gentleman whose family name is that of a famous American shotgun, a friend of the family who ran his pointers three or four times a season as much for the exercise it offered his dogs as for the memories; treasured memories of the quick, full, busy years of youth when turning over twenty coveys of quail in a day's hunting meant little more than a comfortable number of birds to drink to at sundown.

To the best of my knowledge there were but seven coveys of quail living on the farm when I bought it; a year later there were fifteen; the following winter twenty-one; and now, as I write, I have counted and marked twenty-five coveys on the map. My original plan was to raise the number of bobwhite quail to saturation point, partly as an exercise in management, partly because it stimulates my dogs' raison d'être, and partly because I was cocksure that by increasing the population I would be doing the birds a favor. Now that

I have settled on the land and lived through a progression of seasons, I better understand the pace and guidelines nature has set for herself on this particular piece of dirt, guidelines that encourage certain endeavors and discourage others. I can improve the habitat by removing or adding to what is already here, but there is nothing that I, or for that matter any man, can do, to impress nature. By saturating the farm with bobwhite quail what I really had in mind was impressing myself and my friends.

On the other hand, I am going to shape this small corner of nature into a vision of what I believe will best glorify its inherent qualities, a sculpturing of the land—heresy to some who would leave nature to her own devices—gardening on a large scale, subjective landscaping for beauty's sake. And, as I like to see as far as my eyes allow, I remove what is diseased, repetitious, or ugly: catfaced, topless, rachitic, stunted, and otherwise suppressed trees that compete with specimens that would otherwise grow strong and relatively straight. To offset this inclination to prune, I plant five times as many trees as I remove, so that one day, unless I go broke in the process, no matter where I stand I will see only what pleases me. When I want ugly I'll drive into town.

In conjunction with this bit of gardening insanity, I do everything short of killing hawks, bobcats, and coyotes (I do set live traps for the nest destroyers such as opossums, raccoons, and skunks) to provide *Colinus virginianus,* visiting turkeys, and the local deer herd with a comfortable place to live. I realize that the culling of predators is subjective, but culling is an everyday aspect of farm life. In every other respect I do my best to offer free bed and board to those animals or birds that migrate to or take up residence on this land.

In the fall and winter I kill a small percentage of my tenants and eat them. Those I don't eat I give to others who do. Nothing is wasted except the money and time it takes to run the operation, and it might be argued that neither is wasted. In my life I have polluted and abused nature and thousands of her residents, and despite this questionable behavior nature has granted me a life of pleasure and unqualified beauty. Now that I have the wherewithal to manage and tend to this farm and the species that live on it, it would be a moral insult not to do so. The more food and cover I plant the more game and nongame species will thrive, the more water holes, the more fish, the more wildlife, the more predators. Small as it may be, I will make this sequestered world of mine revolve with the assurance of time.

Francis Thompson, an English poet, wrote that one could not pick a flower without troubling a star. To be protective of things because they happen to live here is a new experience, one that I am trying to sort out. So far, owning land has made me aware of nature's ingrained patience, of weather and its reign over every action and conversation, of the feel of steel disks cutting new ground, of the stretching noises of growing corn on a warm summer night, of the weight that monotony bears on those who work the earth, of how the simplicity of rural life is unnecessarily complicated to give it weight and importance, and of how grateful I am to have such a canvas on which to create whatever pleases me; a cocoon inside which I live and love and fight my demons. I keep my contact with the outside world to a minimum and my address book thin; my wife, meanwhile, has joined the contemplative order of the Carmelites. Should I wonder why?

So the farmer in me grows an annual crop of wild flying delicacies and the hunter in me harvests a percentage of this fruitage; the businessman in me recognizes a losing proposition and the child in me doesn't give a shit. A long time ago, a hunter said, "Doubtless the good Lord could have made a better game bird than bobwhite, and better country to hunt him in than our Southern States, but equally doubtless he never did." Any other lingering doubts as to the simplistic nature of my endeavors need only be addressed to my dogs.

The tango:
A sad thought that can be danced.
—Carlos Fuentes

Spring

I

The chain of events leading to a late-June hatch of bobwhite quail in northern Florida begins in March, a
month of indecision and longing. Birds that have
lived in communes since the day they were born begin to
wander off, alone or in small groups, escaping from each
other for reasons they don't quite understand. A few weeks
later, by the official start of spring, their perplexities have vanished and the males are doing everything short of slam-dancing to convince a hen, any hen, of their desirability. They act
foolish under the same spell that has provided the males of all
species with a temporary state of grace since the beginning of
time. Bobwhites sing loudly, dance around each other without the slightest regard to predators, strut their seven-ounce

bodies like twenty-pound turkeys, huff, puff, and glow like any other teenager looking for a female to rub up against. This exemplary display of male hormones begins in late February and lasts until each bird finds a mate, gets eaten, or steps into his sophomore year a virgin.

In March, however, failure is not an issue. Alone by choice for the first time in his precocious life, the bobwhite is free to do as he pleases, and what pleases him is to bandy his weight around looking for a cheap investment by clambering up on logs and stumps from where he bares his breast, taunts his rivals, and, with the delivery of a diminutive Pavarotti, screams his needs like a jackdaw. When the sun sets, like the put-upon poet he knows himself to be, he revels in the pain of yearning.

This behavior, unwise in terms of survival, is non-negotiable in terms of glands. It's a good thing quail speed along on skinny legs and have learned how to squeeze a nine-inch frame into a three-inch opening, because this boisterous conduct, indulged by the females, is nothing more than a mess call to the predator corps.

Predation is most effective when the woods are brown and gray and the stumps are black, the clay wet and the footing treacherous on any given day. In March, when the natural world emerges from winter hungry, a high percentage of each species is earmarked for fodder, and the simple laws of nature don't condone bravado. If anything, the imbecilic behavior of courting birds is programmed to simplify the jobs of their enemies at a time when food is imperative to the survival of themselves and their young. As spring progresses, the task of the hunter is made easier yet by legions of new births. The young and tender of one species feed the young and tender of another, and like musical scales, nature, when left to her own devices, is programmed to achieve a balance between the eaters and the eaten. In March, raptor predation is at its peak, and the accipiters—Cooper's and sharp-shinned hawks—dart from the branches of dead trees and skim noiselessly over the fawn-colored broom sedge worrying the disconnected bobwhites of spring.

Full-grown coyotes run out of the safety of woodlots and across open ground in response to my turkey calls, coyotes I never see at any other time of the year. In April an alligator took up residence in my pond, and I watched it drag under the surface a six-week-old gosling, the only gosling on the pond. By the time I took aim, its parents had seemingly forgotten the mishap and returned to the business of preening. That night I sautéed a slab of the alligator's tail in garlic and butter. I didn't like it—not so much because it had no taste but because I had the gosling in mind, stuffed with shallots and prunes.

Spring welcomes migrating hawks from southern Florida, Cuba, and South America. Some haven't tasted quail since November, and unlike the soaring hawks that are deliberate and slow, these birds are intemperate and quick: bobwhites' main avian nemesis. In their nocturnal hunts, owls undoubtedly reap the rewards of the quail's independence and of its newly found solitary roosting habits, habits that for the other 75 percent of the year concentrate and shape coveys into saucers of bodies the size of hubcaps. Side by side on the ground, the small round birds fight for position, jamming their bodies into a genetic wheel of life that offers security and warmth. From there they face the dangers of darkness as a unit of thirty-odd eyes, some open, some closed. Communally they flush their last meal into neat piles between their heels. In the spring, bobwhites do without the assistance of auxiliary eyes and live precariously between the thrills of courtship and the anguish of being coveted as a special on the menu. Only a minute percentage of wild birds survive until old age. Though you might see the same bobwhite for three springs, the average life expectancy of a quail is eight months, that of a Cooper's hawk one year.

II

I took ownership of the farm in March 1990, but two months earlier, with only a handshake as collateral, the owner, a diminutive sixty-five-year-old Southern belle endowed with the energy of three women half her age and answering to the fine name of Fanny Malone, allowed me to work her land. Her faith in my word, at a time in history when such things are considered at best naive, was remarkable both because of the value of her property and because the work I proposed included planting 22,000 trees in fields where corn had always been sown, cutting down every strand of barbed wire on the place, gutting outbuildings to make room for tractors, grading new roads, and running lit firepots through her woods. Not once during those months did she question my reasons, decisions, or, more important, my qualifications. Faith in a person's word is still honored in the South and is one of the most endearing reasons to live here.

The man who made the improvements on the farm possible, and who is responsible, four years later, for the tenfold improvement in the quail habitat, not to mention the quality of my life, is Bill Poppell, a fifty-five-year-old resident of Coon Bottom, Florida, a workaholic middleweight with eighteen-inch arms and gray hair, a man of pride blessed with the ethics of a Jesuit priest.

Bill does everything from purchasing to repairing, from planting to culling, from burning to mowing; he gives reason to believe in miracles, particularly for someone like me who is neither qualified nor ever will be and whose interests in the inner workings of life are intangible and not at all practical. When Bill was fourteen years old and going to school he stood four feet, eleven inches tall and weighed ninety-three pounds. A year later he went to work full-time in the tobacco fields and flourished under the sun. One decade later, after serving in Korea, he stood five foot ten and weighed two hundred and twenty pounds. He said, "One more year in that classroom would have killed me." Bill has the light skeletal frame and heavy muscle mass of a wrestler, and what percentage of strength he has lost to time has been compensated for by willfulness and an intricate array of levers, wedges, pulleys, and come-alongs, essential to men who like working alone. He prides himself on getting the job done right and ahead of schedule. He is a rare wonder to observe.

Bill, like all men who live on and from the land, is pragmatic when it comes to animals. He will tend to a sick horse for three nights without sleep as easily as he will shoot a possum or a coon for eating bird eggs or a crow for stealing corn. His has been a life of hardship and work, beginning when he was seven years old, lugging tobacco leaves for fifty cents a day during weekends and holidays. His has been a life of farming and hunting and getting good at everything he tried his hand at, from tearing a tractor apart to building a house.

Poppell lives in the shade of his hat, doesn't owe any-one anything and is proud of it. He works harder than any man I've ever met, drinks black coffee, chews tobacco, and is addicted to vanilla ice cream. It is a fact that what Bill does he does by choice, exactly as it should be when you're fifty-five years old and have worked your ass off for forty-eight of them. This farm is as much his as it is mine, and I've told him so.

Bill understands land, weather, and the order of things as I understand how to shoot a gun and cook a bird. He tailors my land to my desires while I wander around dreaming up new things for him to do. He tells me when to take my hand off the poison ivy, my foot off the piss ants, and my mouth off the persimmons. He explains why the bush hog blows a blade when I try to turn the oak stump into wood chips; he pulls my tractor out of the bogs I blunder into, breaks down the nitrogen, phosphate, and potash numbers found in fertilizer, names the wild grasses and flowers that share the land, points out which ears of corn are sweet by the color of the tassels, tells me odd stories about the little people who land on earth on summer nights and leave behind telltale rings of charred grass, and of holes that cannot be filled on waning moons. But best of all he is patient with the mistakes I need to make in order to learn.

Bill sees life as a series of causes and effects and he is practical in his approach to life and work. As the farm's hired gun he protects my sensibilities by dealing quietly with the disagreeable task of predator control and leaves all shapes and forms of reverie to me. Illusions conjure mistakes, and mistakes in his world are costly in terms of time and money and quite often pain. The romance of rural life is best left to those who don't actually handle shovels for a living.

III

When the yellow jessamine flowers swell the fence-rows and the swamps are laced with honeysuckle vines, everyone in the county knows that it is only a matter of time before the fires begin. The day following the end of quail season—the first week in March—white smoke rises and drifts over tens of thousands of acres of southern Georgia and northern Florida forests. The wind moves the smoke that rises from the burning earth in great white sheets across the countryside, and one cannot help but think of the Civil War, of Sherman's army, and of the thousands of small critters incapable of getting out of harm's way. For them, it is war; for the hundreds of species that otherwise would strangle under the suffocating accumulation of Southern vegetation,

relief is at hand. Simply put, the number of dead box turtles I
see after burning is inconsequential compared to the number
of turtles that without fire would starve.

Ten years ago my introduction to controlled burns
involved dropping napalm from a helicopter on five hundred
acres of land bordering the city limits of Tallahassee, land
leased to me by my cousin, a good man who appreciates a hot
fire.

The pilot of the two-man French Hirondelle helicopter was a fast-talking redhead from New Zealand, where
helicopters are kin to bicycles. He stirred the napalm in a
fifty-gallon drum with a broomstick until it thickened and
moved with a life of its own. From the drum he bucketed the
brew into holding tanks fastened to the Hirondelle's belly. He
told me that he was just back from Alabama, where he had
fired 27,000 acres of planted pines for a lumber company and
hadn't been to bed in two days. By then my cousin had called
the Forestry Department for a burning permit, conveniently
forgetting to mention that we planned to nuke the suburbs of
Tallahassee from the sky. When the Hirondelle's side canisters were full of the same mixture the pilot had dropped on
the forests of Southeast Asia twenty years earlier, he stuck his
thumb in the air and we followed it upward, leveling off just
above the steeple of the tallest loblolly pine.

Kiwi let her rip on the upwind border of the property. Molting gobs of napalm, the size of dog turds, fell out of
the canisters to earth; the gobs metamorphosed into tiny orange blemishes on the forest floor, glowing, seconds later,
inside billows of smoke that rose and pursued us.

"Holy shit!" I howled into the speaker. The pilot

raised his thumb again, and I wondered: What if this guy's a fruitcake with a death wish? My hero banked hard and dove into a cloud of black smoke.

It is a fact that, for fear of projectile vomiting, I never once joined my wife or children on a Ferris wheel, but there I was flying up and down in a tin can with steel blades spinning every which direction, sitting on enough firepower to torch the state capitol. The first blast of heat met us head-on and the helicopter bucked thirty feet into the air. "Oh my God," I moaned, feeling my stomach turn over like a summer pond. Thick smoke filled the cockpit. This is it, I thought. Kiwi thinks he's back in Vietnam!

Twenty minutes later we landed next to the soon-to-be-refilled fifty-gallon drum. By then I was so sick I staggered out of the cockpit, waved to my cousin, his wife, and their children, who were anxiously waiting for some quality time in the sky, drove home, and went to bed.

The neighbors called the police, the fire department, two congressmen, and a senator, but they didn't know Cousin Colin, who was not going to be denied the intriguing sight of his land burning from a bird's point of view. He stonewalled the lot of them, shrugged, and said, "A storm in a teacup." I was proud of him and I was proud of the pilot who dropped six loads of napalm without ever crossing a firebreak. He was an ace, a painter of fire.

IV

The practice of burning the pinewoods of the South long predates the arrival of the white man, and by the time the explorers Cabeza de Vaca in 1528 and de Soto a decade later brutalized their way up Florida and southern Georgia, they reported large parklike meadows with widely separated trees, tremendous herds of deer, and rafters of turkey. Those forests had been burned by the natives as far back as 1000 B.C., by Indians of the woodland tradition, and probably by the archaic Indians (8000 B.C.) before them. Fire had been used as a means of opening the woods for travel, of herding and concentrating deer by creating grazing land, of exposing food in the form of acorns and chestnuts to turkeys, and of readying fields for the annual sowing of corn and squash, beans, gourds, and melons.

Francis Willoughby wrote in 1676, "They are like the Spanish Quail, very good and pleasant meat, provided you kill them two or three days before they be rosted and served up. Physicians allow sick persons to eat of their flesh: Neither is there any Fowl among the Indians, next to tame Poultry, whose flesh is to be preferred before it, either for wholsomness or taste. . . . They are kept in Coops, and fed with Indian Wheat and are common in many parts of this Country." A turgid tongue-twister bearing a certain historical weight.

When a Southern hardwood canopy closes, the world below turns dank, the food source changes, and the trees struggle and stretch for the sun's favors, the survivors displaying their resolve with misshapen limbs. In the fall and early winter deer and quail shop in this underworld for acorns. Turkeys, by nature more opportunistic, add crawfish and lizards to the list. In general, bobwhites prefer habitat photosynthetically fertilized by the sun, with trees far enough apart to cast individual shadows on a floor where the ground cover grows like a quilt: dense in some places and thin in others. Bobwhites like to feel dirt between their toes and are not equipped to scratch under matted cover for food. They relish pine seed, berries from dogwood trees, crab apples, and the odd acorn. By the end of winter, when the hard seeds, green growth, and mast have been gleaned, fire magically opens a new, snug reserve of food that for months had been sifting through pine needles and dying grasses to the forest floor; roasted treasures immediately accessible to all grain-eating birds, squirrels, and deer. Heat blisters the hard-shelled seeds of legumes such as partridge peas, beggarweed, and lespedeza, which until then were hibernating underground. Scarified back to life, these seeds resume their genetic aspiration to grow and multiply, and, in the case of legumes, develop into prime sources of food, cover, and bugging grounds for quail and turkey alike.

In 1931, when both governmental agencies and privately employed foresters totally excluded the use of fire in the woods, a nucleus of biologists, funded by a group of industrialists and wealthy southern Georgia and northern Florida landowners headed by Herbert L. Stoddard, published *The Bobwhite Quail: Its Habits, Preservation and Increase,* a book that anyone even vaguely interested in bobwhite quail should own because it is still, and always will be, the Gideon Bible of quail management.

Stoddard's five-year study included the use of fire both as a means of improving the habitat—hence increasing the quail population—and as a method of improving the commercial production of timber. It is said that foresters were so set against fire that the first time Stoddard publicly praised its benefits he was booed off the stage by his peers. Nevertheless, Stoddard's research and application of fire in the Southern woods eventually convinced the timber industry that burning every fourth or fifth year, a decade or so after the pine saplings were planted, reduced the hazard of wildfires, notorious for terminating thirty-year investments in minutes.

The application of a hot summer sun on a pine-forest floor provokes a growth reaction unique to the Southeast. No other forest in the country is blessed with such a rich, diversified, and permanent undergrowth, perfectly located and adapted to overwinter migratory birds. The downside to this lush evolution is that, left unchecked for five years, the under-story grows into grasses, vines, and pine straw tangles, walls of dead vegetation so dense and constricting that they are unfit for all but a handful of species. The slow progression from fields to pine trees to an eventual climax hardwood forest promotes a steady ground-floor progression from grass and weed to an impenetrable deciduous jungle.

From a wildlife-management point of view, fire cleans and retards the growth of ground litter and hardwood saplings. From a forestry point of view, controlled burns control a dry, overgrown source of fuel yearning for a match.

Those who do not want nature modified in any way, particularly not for the benefit of specific species, feel that the biological development of the planet is a continuous mutation of life, encouraged by natural occurrences as tedious as the advance and retreat of glaciers and as rapid as the eruption of a volcano. Species that do not adapt to one ecosystem adapt to another or disappear. They are right, but the questions arise: What do you want and what are you willing to give up? No management program can serve all needs, much less all species. Without fire the pine forests of the Southeast would revert to hardwoods. So, if we are to return to nature, how far back do we go? This specific ecosystem was historically groomed through the propagation of wildfires, first from lightning and later by the Indians. In this day and age, wildfires present unacceptable dangers to human and animal life and, more pragmatically, unacceptable losses to the timber industry. Since we have physically altered the geography of nature by moving hundreds of millions of our own species into a system finely tuned to celestial tides and the whims of physics but impotent in the face of man's insults and relentless desecration, it would seem appropriate that we manage what we have altered and clean up what we have soiled. We cannot buy plywood without cutting trees any more than we can delight in nature without giving something back.

In this case, the opposition surrounding controlled burning stems first and foremost from man's primeval terror of fire and secondly from the fact that smoke is a pollutant—regardless that it is a natural phenomenon and, compared quantitatively to what rises from our cities daily, a nonissue. A more practical reason for opposing controlled burning comes not from the radical right or left but from the ornithological community, where there is mounting concern that extensive pine management will affect the lives of millions of new tropical songbirds that migrate up from the rain forests of Central America looking for the junglelike habitat we work so diligently to clear.

All these issues warrant a great deal of thought by both interested and uninterested parties. Population volatility and the shift from rural to city life disallow absolute solutions to the interaction between humans and nature. Those whose livelihoods depend on timber are going to side with those who own the timber. Those who love nature for its own sake are unswayed by scientific rhetoric. That leaves the majority of mankind, which doesn't give a damn one way or the other, a handful of professionals who care, and a minority of amateurs like me.

Climax grasses, such as broom sedge, spread quickly and choke fallow fields in a few years, surrendering them to cotton rats, which relish the density. The rats in residence are overseen by battalions of predators that would just as soon eat a quail as a rodent. Fire opens that overgrowth just as it opens the floor of the forest, allowing bobwhites to travel the edges and use what second-year broom sedge escaped the fire as nesting cover. A percentage of what is burned is harrowed in the late spring, giving the sun a clean place to rest and renew the vegetative process. In June, year-old corn stalks, sorghum, and innumerable islands of unburned grass still totter in the breeze, a force to be reckoned with and a fine place for a quail to lay an egg. It seems that old grass, like old people, takes a long time to die.

V

I stop hunting around the middle of February, when instead of finding coveys my dogs point singles and pairs. No matter what anyone says, our quail-hunting season is too long (three and a half months) for the good of the species. The joys of hunting I experienced in September erode over the months, and by February I am loath to pull the trigger on anything that breathes. Each season has its priorities, and by the end of winter mine turn to growing things. The irony, of course, is that if I want to grow strong trees and provide a plentitude of food and safe habitat for my boarders, I have to promote an interaction between organisms—both vegetal and animal—and their environment (specifically, the science of ecology). In the Southeast, that means setting fire to the land.

Firing a section of woods, particularly if you own or are responsible for them, awakens something old and fearful in man, like a great windstorm or a close accident. I have been mixing fuel for a decade now, at a ratio of three parts diesel to one part gasoline, into four-gallon firepots, and have set thousands of acres on fire. But every spring, particularly the first morning, I do so with the innate feeling that I am disobeying a fundamental rule, a rule repeated over and over to me by my mother as far back as I can remember: "Do not play with fire!" And therein lies part of the fascination. Scientific benefits aside, there is something visceral and unknown about cracking a match that gathers a man's testicles like only a glance at death or the promise of sex ever does.

Fire licks the disease off the trunks of pine trees and, if properly applied, kills enough lower branches for the trees to grow tall and without rickets. The heat clears the woods of ticks, chiggers, and other parasites, as well as bark-boring beetles, which home in on a scent emanated by weak or wounded pines and destroy the tree in a matter of days. Resin, acting like a salve, flows out of crippled pine trees, and if the bugs don't find it the fire usually does, branding the hot resin into black catfaces in the thick, multilayered bark. The catface brands spread every year, burying deeper and deeper into the soft wood, slowly breaking its resilience, until one day the tree falls and rots and mushrooms grow, and the process of life starts over again.

Bill plows firebreaks around the perimeters of those sections of woods left unburned the year before (I burn 50 percent of the farm every year, in increments of five to twenty acres). A master tractor operator, Bill is at his best tap-dancing on the pedals of the clutch and brakes. I set the fires while he pushes over logs and stumps, crowds the flames, and spins the harrow blades over potential problems. During it all he furiously works over a huge plug of chew. This bit of legal speed, coupled with coffee chasers, keeps him wired until he gets home to his double-wide, where he spoons a quart of vanilla ice cream into his mouth to ease his weakened stomach—a personal approach to checks and balances.

On a clear and cool March morning a couple of years ago, with the wind out of the north at eight miles an hour, we fired the bottoms on the eastern boundaries of the farm. I'd hoped to burn about a hundred acres that day, but the wind never stood still long enough for a plan to work. We began by firing a block of planted pines with two years' worth of cones and needles on the ground. Just about the time our carefully set backfire eased forward, the wind turned, swirling the pine tops and fueling the fire into an unwanted rage, the heat shriveling the undergrowth ahead of the flames. The smoke turned black, and the flames swirled into orange-colored funnel clouds. We were lucky that the fire stopped when it reached the break; it stopped just as suddenly as it had started, leaving in its path mature pine trees with trunks scorched twenty feet high, dead hardwood trees whose thinner bark had collapsed under the heat, and, where the fire had moved the fastest, perfectly shaped, white-tipped blades of black grass.

The smell of pine heart burning is distinct and addictive, a stickiness that coats the air for weeks. Along with diesel fuel, burning pine heart releases an odor one shouldn't forget from one year to the next; but for reasons I don't quite understand, I always do. The first time I crack a match, my brain shrieks and revolts. A week later I don't want the smell of pinesap to ever go away.

That afternoon we backfired a block of young pine trees. The fire skulked away from the wind like an ebbing tide, a tiny red wave five inches high scorching the earth, weaving in and out of the crooks and crannies of years of debris, leaving behind a uniform blanket of soot. Backfires are as fascinating to me as their counterparts, the rolling headfires that suck the air out of gopher holes and hurl flames beyond the smoke and fear all the way up to where the sky is blue. The first fire cleans; the latter kills. Both have a place in woodland management, but unless the burn is to destroy dense stands of saplings, or is called for by reasons of time versus acreage, I prefer the former because of its contemplative, quiet progress.

Afternoon clouds pushed long shadows over the blackened earth. The fire had barely singed the meager litter of leaves under the oak trees and had halted at the strips of annual rye and winter wheat I'd sowed back in November; there, green ribbons of grass waved in the breeze, undaunted by my devices. Meanwhile, because spring was on the way, the live oak leaves that had survived winter had turned yellow and brown from the heat.

When the fires were out, the stumps on the side of the shadowed slopes smoldered into a gray world of bats and owls. Just before dark I saw a woodcock rise out of a burned creek bottom, outlined against a silver sky; the bird looked fake, a freeze-frame picture of nature projected onto a canvas, traced by an impersonator. Diesel fuel lingered on my skin, oily, determined, and unaffected by soap. Soot clung to my boots and smoke had parched my eyes. At the house I built myself a big drink. My daughter called it a killer drink. She was right.

I had been reminded again how quickly a fickle wind can turn a creeping backfire into a maelstrom, and how heat races up hills and creeps down hollows, but mainly I learned about the lay of my land, its vulnerability to errors, and most of all about its finiteness.

The strange irregularities and texture of the earth are apparent when a rain follows a burn. The earth is hard, strewn with mortified limbs and treetops, logs, smoking stumps that refuse to rot, shriveled leaves in a motif of black on black. Rain sinks the potash and minerals into the ground and drags the surplus to the creek bottoms. It washes color back into the face of darkness and exposes the red clay domes of thousands upon thousands of anthills, on the slopes, in the wood, the hollows, everywhere. Nature is at her most naked after a burn, and like a molting bird, she's both vulnerable and risible, if one feels like laughing.

Two weeks later—sometimes sooner, depending on rain, nighttime temperatures, and dew—the land greens up. Miniature fingers of chlorophyll stipple the earth, and these first revelations of color, pinned on shadowy backgrounds, deepen the landscape.

Six weeks beyond that, the minerals that have sifted into the earth, the scarification of dormant seeds, the rains, and the hot sun have joined forces to introduce a vegetable explosion. When the woods still smell of resin, the ephemeral rainbow of wildflowers hurries to live and die before the canopy fills with leaves and casts shadows on their parade. It is said that the appearance of flowers coincided with the mystifying emergence of man on earth. Lupines and coral beans, violets, azaleas, redbuds, and wild green onions are everywhere. Insects multiply in the lush evolution of legumes and contribute protein and minerals to the health of nesting hens and their eggs and later to the growth of turkey poults and bobwhite fledglings during the summer months. White-tailed does and their fawns consume the beans of the same legumes in the fall.

I alter the circle of life and death on my land every year. I believe it is for the better. Perhaps I am wrong; perhaps I am right. Rachel Carson wrote, "The control of nature is a phrase born in arrogance," and while I am perfectly aware that what I do is a form of arrogance, I would suggest that given the decimation of habitat in all parts of the world, she might forgive me for playing God on an eight-hundred-acre farm.

In the long run it makes no difference; short of nuclear holocaust, the earth will outlive this present set of species, including man. Regardless, my heart goes out to the creatures that aren't nimble enough to avoid death on those days when I walk the woods with fire dripping from my fingers. I look at the empty shells of box turtles and armadillos, the ashes of skunks, hook-shaped and white against the pitch-black earth, and I feel remorse for them and the thousands of crawling creatures that blew away in the updraft of my tempest. But it is a short sorrow; death came and went quickly over my land, and unlike most modern disasters, this ending is as old as the planet and leaves behind, if not solace for the sentient ones that perished, at least faith and a future for those that survived.

VI

Nature's production of wild food, which is at its natural low in February, has by April shifted into second gear. Warm nights and warmer days unlock pollen and release to the wind a pale, green mist. Oak trees stand behind gossamer veils of budding leaves, the pubescent flowers of the wisteria vines mantle fences and host trees, wild grasses stretch out of the lukewarm earth to accommodate and protect the insect hatch. Redheaded woodpeckers drill into the trunks of pine trees, delivering them of sap, which flows like an apron of lava, a girdle of glue retarding the progression of snakes to the birds' nests.

I watched an osprey pluck a rat snake off a limb at the very crown of an eighty-foot loblolly pine. A mockingbird took offense and pestered the hawk until it dropped its catch. I searched for it, but the snake's bungee cord body had absorbed the fall, and it was gone. I then looked straight up to where it had fallen from and delighted at the resolve of an appetite that would shimmy that far for an egg.

The ratio of male to female bobwhite quail is six to five in favor of the males, thus encouraging competition for breeding rights; numbers good for perpetuating the gene pool, less good for one out of six males. The hens, who are not as anxious to breed as their counterparts, concentrate on gaining the weight and building the strength necessary to fashion nests, lay and incubate a dozen or more eggs, protect and rear the broods, and survive the process, which begins as early as March and ends as late as November, when family groups disperse and intermingle with each other.

It is April, and the bobwhites have been singing for two weeks. I see them on every log, eyes glazed, beaks open, singing out in an unconscious world of moist dreams, chattering nerve cells, and female cloacas. The hens in turn display a soft spot for those bobwhites that exhibit a strong paternal instinct, as incubating the clutch and caring for the hatchlings is the ticket to nirvana. Quail are about as monogamous as humans. If the opportunity for a little aside presents itself, *pourquoi pas?* But in general the couple work out whatever differences birds encounter and raise their brood together. One would assume that a hen grants a male access to her favors because of his strength, his beauty, or his aggressiveness, and I'm sure that it happens, but last spring I watched three cock birds jousting with one another while the object of their desire stood demurely in a thicket, a few yards away, seemingly paying no attention to the goings-on. One bird was being bullied by the other two, and after having been run off half a dozen times, took refuge under a pine top and resigned himself to the role of spectator. The two remaining birds faced off, blew up their feathers, lowered their heads, and chased each other like billy goats. The contest eventually took them out of sight behind a large oak tree, a signal for the spectator bird to emerge from under his branch and run to the thicket as fast as his short legs would take him. There, he stood inches in front of his paramour, tilting his head this way and that, showing off his colors. To his utter joy and astonishment, I'm sure, the hen squatted on the ground, twisted her tail feathers out of his way, and allowed him to mount her. Or so I think, because all I saw of this adherence of organs was a momentary flutter of wings. When the louts returned from battling each other, the chosen one ran them off.

I like to think that my seven-ounce hero charmed his hen by using his wits, but regardless of my fantasy, studies indicate that once a male successfully covers a hen, his confidence is such that he will successfully defend his tenure from all interlopers. Although the consensus of opinion is that couples are monogamous, I have also observed some less-than-devoted conduct on the part of hens openly encouraging display behavior from males other than their mates. It seems that if promiscuity there is, it originates with the female of the species. However, in this day and age, polyandry is a state of affairs best left alone.

In the case of the single male, his lusting and pining continues. For those unchosen males the priority is still to con a hen the only way they know how: by whistling one up. But as the season progresses and hens become scarce, the bachelors can only covet what they don't have and hope for the death of a rival. The birds that sang so longingly in March forget the refrain by September.

For those birds that have found each other, the consideration is to pick a site and build a nest. In the first instance, and I assume after much bird talk, some couples merely fill a depression in the earth with grass, pine straw, and leaves, while others add a roof and an entranceway to their home. In either case, quail like to nest on the edges of unrelated habitat, such as next to a road or field or a freshly harrowed firebreak, preferably close to food. A good management practice is to leave a hundred-foot-wide strip of rough on either side of all dirt roads for nesting cover. Later, when the breeding season is over, those strips of rough can be left as is, mowed, or harrowed-in and planted in a late season cover crop such as clover or rye.

The loss rate of hens during incubation is higher than at any other time of the bird's adult life, and it is this vulnerability to predation that accounts for the lopsided ratio of five hens to six males observed the rest of the year. A pair of skunks working a fencerow at night will eat every single egg they come across, as well as what birds they catch napping. Studies show that 50 percent of quail nests are destroyed by weather, predation, or man, and although bobwhites do rebuild their nests until they are successful or run out of time, the clutches grow progressively smaller with each attempt.

The average clutch for a bobwhite quail in the Southeast is fourteen eggs, of which most hatch, but only 50 percent of the hatchlings celebrate their two-week birthday.

From that original clutch of fourteen eggs, six will live to see the leaves turn. Not a percentage to brag about, but one that does explain why such little birds lay so many eggs.

When the weather is good, hens lay an egg a day until the clutch is complete. During that time I see pairs of bobwhites all over the farm, and I know that somewhere, hidden under a pine top or inside a clump of dead grass, a nest awaits its daily deposit. I follow paired birds to their nest sometimes and, careful not to touch anything, return when they are feeding elsewhere. Every day I count a new off-white-colored egg, but I have never seen a bird of any kind lay one, except a chicken once, when I was young and lived on a farm in France. The hen grunted (or so I like to remember) and pecked at my hand when I removed her investment from the straw. I wiped the egg on my shirt, piped two small holes at opposite ends with my knife, and sucked the slippery warmth down my throat, like all farm boys did in those days.

VII

April 19, 1992 (Easter Day)

Bill says, "It is best to cut a hog on a falling moon. It keeps the bleeding down." We cut two boar hogs today. Pigs out of a sow trapped six months earlier in Reed Swamp. We bred her to a Georgia boar and I have been feeding these swine corn and kitchen scraps ever since the day the sow built herself a mattress of dog fennel, hid underneath it, and dropped a litter of eight young ones. We turned the piglets and their mother out in the woods for a month to flavor them up, so to speak, lost two gilts to coyotes, and trapped the rest back in order to cut the boars and fatten them. I will have them butchered next month and they will weigh between forty and fifty pounds, dressed.

Bill's brother, Jerry, who is in the pig business, came by early, before church, and after telling me that every inch of a pig makes fine eating—from the rooter to the pooter—sent his black helper into the pen. The short, stocky man, whose scars attested to a number of mistakes, moved like a dancer and herded the pigs into a corner. When it was right for him, he snatched a young boar by one ear, tipped it over, and, taking hold of a ham hock, handed seventy pounds of pig, effortlessly, upside down and screaming, over the railing. Bill set the boar hog on its back into an open-ended metal funnel with its head completely enclosed in an iron cone. Jerry cut down the middle of the pig's scrotum, fished out the testicles one at a time with his forefinger, severed the canals, dropped the fruits of his work, and squirted the incision with menthol. Back in the pen, the barrow huddled in a corner, screaming louder than ever, until it spotted its nuts in the wallow and ate them. Neither he nor a second pig bled a drop. A sign of moonbeams and dexterity.

Later that day it rained on the farm for the first time in weeks. Almost half an inch, enough to clean off the grass, the air, and the plowed earth. Bill planted corn off and on until seven P.M. He went home but returned to the fields three times after the pigs were cut, once after church and twice between rain showers. He plants our corn with old mule planters he jury-rigged to pull behind the tractor. He sows in low gear, as anything higher flings the seeds past the slots out of which they are intended to fall. The exactness of planting corn while sitting on a tractor in front of a planter built to be used while walking behind a mule is demanding and antiquated, but it works. The rows are straight and true, just as the farmer in Bill wants them to be. I watch him from my office and wish he drank so I could offer him some whiskey. During a break he tells me that when he was a kid he used to peel the bark off of young sweet gums, wait a day or two, scrape the resin, mix it with some of his mother's flour, and chew it while he worked, instead of gum, which cost a penny. Bill spins the tractor back on track and says, "Hell, it wasn't nothing but sap and worm shit." The light now is bright and yellow around the tractor; the earth turns black behind the planters.

VIII

J im Buckner is a tall, dark-haired man, soft-spoken and knowledgeable in the way that all wildlife biologists (in his case forester-biologist) should be. Many of his peers conveniently forget, a decade or so into their careers, that life and the study of life begin in the field, and that while extrapolating data is a necessity, the gathering of that material is the art. The window through which a quail, for example, looks at the world can be measured in inches and angles; what it sees cannot be read on a chart. Managing a species or an ecosystem is an unstable alliance between the technocrats and the gatherers. Those who choose to live and die behind a desk have in effect taken the position of pontificators. Buckner is from the school of "hands-on" management, at the crossroads of science and art. The fundamental accountability of research is in the sharing of knowledge, and Jim obliges with grace.

A hundred or so thousand years ago, when we inherited the extra gene or two that differentiated us from our first cousin the chimpanzee, we became the best killing machines on the planet. Our greater skills and intelligence were no match for the animals we coveted, and we coveted them all. The extinction of every great mammal during the years following our emergence out of Africa coincides closely with our arrival on each of the remaining continents. A hundred years ago we plucked the feathers off egrets to make hats for our wives; now we spray our armpits and tear open the heavens while slowly but surely the developers cement the earth to the sky.

It is naive of me, I know, but I always assume that regardless of our specific talents and differences, hunters, naturalists, biologists, animal lovers, and the multitude of organizations that profess to revere and delight in the natural world are all working, by choice, for a cast of characters so utterly dependent on our compassion and decisions that self-aggrandizement and vanity within these factions is as inconceivable as it is when dealing with starving children. I am wrong in both cases, of course. At best, the competing powers within the various communities can be blamed for indulging in "the narcissism of small differences"; at worst they are politicians. "An oyster held too close to the eye obscures the view of the rest of the world," is the polite way Herbert L. Stoddard put it. Being less polite and more militant than Herbert L., I find the word that best fits my opinion of these small men with large egos is assholes.

Buckner, however, is in the field four or five hours a day, five days a week, and the remarks that leave his mouth ring with the quiet confidence of a professional too wise and circumspect to second-guess nature's ways.

I rode on the tire guard of a tractor next to Buckner while he drew an entire landscape with a six-foot-wide harrow. He cut my two-hundred-acre, L-shaped field into long slices of red clay where, in his mind's eye, he could already see rows of pine trees growing. At first it didn't make sense, but after he had raised and dropped the harrow a few times, the ribbons of freshly turned dirt began to take on a shape and life of their own. I realized that what had seemed like aimless meanderings were in fact geometrical strokes that bisected and trisected sections of this enormous field in patterns firmly embedded in his head. Jim used the wet-weather ponds and the handful of solitary oaks and ironwoods that pepper the field as landmarks. To deter erosion he clung to the contour of the terrain, explaining while he harrowed that during the fourth or fifth winter I would have to pick and choose the best loblolly pines, mow down the poor specimens, and prune the lower limbs of the remaining trees at eye-level to stop them from spreading horizontally. The work involved in pruning the limbs off thousands of pine trees was mind-boggling then, and getting worse as the time grows nearer.

Jim worked the natural profile of the land, drawing lines that pleased his eye while accomplishing the goal of turning an empty sea of grass into a future maze of long, narrow fields framed by rows of tall trees. We were in fact building a landscape reminiscent of some of the classic gardens of Europe, except on a much larger scale. And instead of planting slow-developing evergreens such as yew trees and boxwoods, we Americans had opted for fast-growing softwoods. This topiary was not being designed so much for the sake of the gentry as for the contemplation of high-flying birds and the pleasure of those that would land in it.

While we were on the tractor, Buckner outlined the habits of the game that would be drawn to the farm, the vagaries of the weather, the plants and seeds best suited for the loamy soil of the region, and always returned to one statement: "In this business, there are no givens. Nothing is predictable. The name of the game is experiment."

Since that day, and in subsequent years of tinkering with this earth, I have watched plum trees thrive in one place and others die, six feet away. I have moved pitiable food patches by as little as ten yards and watched them flourish. And I have stubbornly planted trees in the holes where other trees had died and watched the new ones expire just as quickly. A French viticulturist friend, justifying the greatness of his wine, told me, "First, it is a matter of soil, then a matter of history, and finally a matter of love."

A few days after Jim traced the clay, a large truck full of seedlings—followed by a flatbed, a tractor, and a transplanter that looked like an antiquated metal sulky with a three-point hitch, a blade, cogwheels, metal slots, a very uncomfortable-looking bicycle seat, and a single, offset rubber tire—made its way up to the barn. The tractor, driven by a well-fed white man, set out after Buckner's harrowed ground towing the planter, in which five hundred loblolly seedlings were stacked within arm's reach of a much thinner black man sitting on a dried-out leather seat. The leading blade of the transplanter dug a shallow furrow into which each seedling was hand-delivered via a narrow metal holder soldered to a motorcycle chain, calibrated to plant a pine tree every six feet. The rows were four trees wide and ten feet apart, leaving plenty of room for Bill to mow between them without skinning bark.

It was a meticulous and boring job for the tractor driver and a real backbreaker for the man setting the seedlings as he bounced across anthills, tractor ruts, and gopher holes. Counting the field in question plus four smaller ones, the black man planted twenty-two thousand pine trees in three days, the disks between his vertebrae serving as sole shock absorbers.

I could have joined a government program that would have supplied me with both pine trees and the cost of planting them, in an effort to control erosion and reforest some of the millions of acres it had encouraged to be over-timbered during the past century. It is (for once) a good program, but I had just informed the Agriculture Stabilization and Conservation Service (ASCS) office that I intended to let the fields grow fallow and much to my stupefaction had been told that I was entitled to huge dollar allotments for not (!) growing corn or wheat for profit. Being new to the game I took the money and began my life as a "farmer" by doing nothing. After the third visit from one of the two agencies concerned I realized that if I wanted to keep my privacy (the only reason for owning unproductive land) I had better shut my mouth, turn down every subsidy dreamed up by a government that at the core of its policy-making is either venal or unconscious, and mind my own business. So I planted my own trees.

IX

The seven or eight coveys of quail that lived on the farm when I bought it in 1990 represented the average number of birds, give or take, that had been living there since the land had been actively managed for hunting twenty-five years earlier. To increase those numbers I needed to do three things: plant permanent food/cover patches; plant annual food/cover plots; and—my only real headache in terms of quail management—remove as much Pensacola Bahia grass (originally brought in from South America to fight erosion on the beaches of northeastern Florida, and later used for hay) as possible. The two-hundred-acre field had been planted in corn for so long that the problems would not appear until the following year, in the shape of common Bermuda grass, another invading herb planted for forage thirty years before when Brahma cattle roamed the plantation. The fields, pasture, and woodlots had endured the defecation of a thousand intestines and the weight of four times as many hooves, the former propagating undigested grass seeds and the latter packing those seeds into the ground to a depth and hardness that challenged the sharpest chisel plow.

Bill and I began by removing miles of old barbed wire (usually embedded into trees, etc.), but faced with the logistics of more than two hundred acres of unwanted grass, I hired a professional to spray the fields with herbicides. I despise chemicals more than I do *Bos taurus primigenius* (cows), but my choices were limited; untended Pensacola grass grows so thick that except during the nesting season no sensible quail would think of navigating beyond its edges for fear of a terminal anxiety attack.

Another tractor arrived, this time pulling a five-hundred-gallon herbicide sprayer soon to be filled with a mixture of Roundup, mineral oil (to help the Roundup stick to the grass), and water. For a day and a half it crisscrossed the fields and pastures at a set speed, booms extended like the wings of a toy plane, discharging at forty pounds of pressure per acre gallons of misty poison and killing every living plant in its path. Or so I thought. A week later, the blue-green fields of April had turned brown: ungulate brown.

We were then advised to harrow and cross-harrow the sprayed fields, which we did ad nauseam, to finely chop what was left of the roots. Back and forth we harrowed for hundreds of hours, back and forth across the brown earth, feeling nothing—the mind set in that terminal condition of cruise control that is familiar to farmers the world over—cutting the fields into minute herringbones until all the furrows were straight and the earth powder-soft.

As if that weren't enough, three of the toughest fields were completely turned upside down by Bill and his bottom plows, two enormous pieces of steel that stand like upside-down shark fins and dig so deep they flip angleworms into the maws of waiting crows. These great chunks of earth were left to bake for two months and then had to be painfully harrowed smooth again. A year later, 80 percent of the Pensacola Bahia grass was back.

Meanwhile, smudges of Bermuda grass started showing up in the two-hundred-acre field. By harrowing-in food plots and planting pine trees, the mat grass that had been shadowed by corn for years was making a strong comeback, in effect thanking us for reintroducing it to the sun. A rainy season later, broad patches the size of basketball courts slinked across the field like fungus, and if Pensacola Bahia grass discourages quail, Bermuda grows so rank it discourages even my dogs.

This time we bought our own sprayer, the chemicals and oil to fill it, nuked the Bahia all over again, and tried spot-killing the worst patches of Bermuda. We hoped that what evolved behind the chemicals would shade what grass we didn't kill. The nightmare continued as what came up were tall, dense stands of coffee weeds and nothing else. Back into the fields we went, this time loaded with 2, 4-D amine, a carcinogenic chemical that only kills broadleaf plants. Bill wore a mask, goggles, and a suit that made his life, inside of it, hell. Six weeks later, Johnson grass (not a favorite of quail but at least attractive to me), sand spurs, and Crotalaria popped out of the exhausted earth. One year later the Bermuda grass was back.

I have always hated ungulates for the cavalier manner in which they were allowed to eat so much of the West; now I hate them for what they did to this land. As for the herbicides, I have put most of this chemical nightmare to rest. It would take years of spraying to undo what was planted in good faith for reasons other than my own, and since I no longer plan to spend all my efforts producing a quail utopia, I have restructured my burning program. I'll burn some problem areas later, when the grass has started to grow, in effect stunting it and retarding its development. In other problem areas I won't burn at all for three or four years, effectively promoting a hardwood growth that will shade out or certainly diversify the mat grasses. In the winter I harrow small fields within larger fields, turning under the areas where the Bermuda grass grows rankest and planting them in winter wheat and clover, in effect retarding the noxious growth with a source of spring food and summer nesting cover.

I thought for a while that I could return to this land its original plants and native grasses, the same vegetation that thrived during the tenure of the Lower Creek Indians. That will not happen. Cow fodder, imported into the country as a solution to a problem (not really all that different from what I do when I plant Kobe Lespedeza or Egyptian wheat), whipped my ass. The best I can hope for is that the natural progression of weeds will come and go with the seasons until one day, five or ten years down the road, the fields will climax in broom sedge and shade out the grass. The real value of broom sedge to quail will be as nesting sites and escape cover, and it is amusing to note that soon after the sedge waves tall and golden in the autumn winds it will be time to plow huge chunks of it back into the ground, which will enervate the weeds and hardwoods and jump-start the process all over again.

S pring burning followed later by harrowing, before the quail settle onto their nests, are two of the best things a landowner (as long as his land isn't infested with invading mat-type grasses) can do for quail short of planting food and cover. Disturbing the soil promotes legumes and adds miles of new edges for the birds to hug. A man can mount his tractor for a Sunday promenade, drop the harrow and meander through his woods to his heart's content, and do wonders for his game population. If he feels flush, he can spread a little slag or lime on these newly cut trails and six months later retrace his steps by following the lush new growth.

The first year, Buckner had us plant bicolor Lespedeza and plum trees, Lespedeza as a permanent and first-year cover as well as a food source, and plum thickets as a long-range (four- to ten-year) additional food and roosting cover. Both plants grow thick and shade out the ground. This allows their seeds to fall on bare dirt, an energy-saving and reliable method of presenting food to quail, a must in fields that we knew would draw rodents to the grain and raptors to the rodents; fields that would offer very little cover until the pine trees gained stature. We needed as much cover as possible, because it made no sense to draw bobwhites to food simply to feed them to the hawks.

The year-old Lespedeza seedlings were planted on prepared ground in long, narrow 12-by-250-foot strips close to the pine seedlings, and by summer's end quail had taken up residence under their canopies of loose flowering heads. The plum trees were planted by hand as seedlings in groups of fifteen or twenty at the head of each Lespedeza strip. For reasons of managerial continuity, in July we planted rows of sorghum for food and cover, parallel to and about the same size as the Lespedeza patches, so that the coveys could navigate from food to cover with minimum exposure to predation. With very few birds on the property we encouraged optimum habitat in a minimum time span. In all, we planted seventy-two Lespedeza plots—eighteen in the woods, the rest in the fields—for a total of five thousand seedlings. The plum tree total came to one hundred and twenty.

The losses that first year were low in the Lespedeza patches, but heavy in the plum department, mainly as a result of what is becoming characteristic in northern Florida and southern Georgia: a drought that lasted forty-one days and a sun that regularly spun the needle of the tractor-mounted thermometer to 120 degrees Fahrenheit.

We also broadcast brown-top millet on the edges of the roads and planted corn in two ten-acre dove fields and five smaller patches (two acres each) in the open pastures. By law I was not allowed to harvest the grain, as I was being paid not to, but I did anyway, not to sell but to turn out later as a supplement to the deer, turkey, and quail's winter diet. The brown-top offered cover, seeds, and excellent bugging grounds on which the young quail could test their skills. The corn offered tall cover, and of course food until January. We also planted rows of Kobe Lespedeza and broad patches of partridge peas, the former being an accessible annual in terms of cash outlay, the latter being a very expensive perennial. The results were dismal with the former and excellent with the latter. The partridge peas did so well (planted in full sunlight) that I plan to buy a small quantity of seeds over the next four or five years to assure their permanence both as a source of food and for the visual delight of yellow August blooms.

The most interesting article I have read about quail food is "The Value of a Seed," written by Fred S. Guthery, a research scientist at the Kleberg Institute in Texas. Guthery breaks down the caloric value of the quail's more common foods and compares that value to the effort expended in finding the food and to the quantity of seeds it takes to keep a bird alive. Assuming it takes sixty calories of usable energy to keep a bobwhite healthy for one day, here are some of the equations: A bird would have to eat 18,639 common Lespedeza seeds, or 3,605 of my colorful partridge peas, or 1,160 common sunflower seeds, 666 grain sorghum, 648 wheat, 103 soybeans, or 41 kernels of corn. If we take common Lespedeza as an example, and if the bird ate one seed every two seconds, it would take ten hours for it to eat enough to maintain its body weight. Guthery points out that a larger seed usually contains more calories than a small one, so, given a choice, it makes sense to plant food plots that bear large seeds rich in oil. Corn is expensive in terms of time and labor to plant, but as a food source or as a supplement in feeders it cannot be beat.

During the first twelve months of owning the farm, we turned a piece of real estate on which corn was grown in one field, hay was cut in the others, and the woods were burned on the remainder every year for appearance's sake, into a wildlife food mill. By doing so we fed thousands of nongame species. We doubled the coveys of quail, greatly enhanced the number of young turkeys, and drew white-tailed deer from every direction. That year I harvested a token eight quail for the pot. I'm not sure if my discretion in the matter helped—I think I could have killed three times that many birds and still doubled my coveys. In biological terms, in contrast to the food and cover we sowed, this temperate harvest meant nothing; in terms of making me feel good, it meant a lot.

XI

May 28, 1991

A six-foot alligator climbed out of the ditch next to Old Bam-
bridge Road this morning after a soaking squall had passed. It
stopped on the blacktop and did a dozen push-ups before
moving on. Later, two black snakes rose like candelabras from
the grass on the edge of a clay road, weaving around each
other's rippling bodies until, except for two heads looking at
each other, they were one. Turtles were everywhere. It
would seem that there is something about the month of May
that animates reptilian emotions.

By afternoon, pollen gilded the sun and the heat had
driven the moisture back into the clouds. Once again red dirt

rose behind passing cars and clung to the leaves of the road-side trees. I drove past an old white man wearing a straw hat and baggy pants. He hobbled on crutches down the shady side of the road next to a lemon-colored pointer bitch with sagging gray teats. They turned to look at me. In the mirror I saw a pair of quail flush out of the ditch in front of them; the bitch pointed and the man touched her head. I walked three miles around the big field at sunset, walking like a child dreaming, gliding over the ineffable beauty of the earth. A bobwhite with a purple face ducked into a tangle of dewberries. My dog returned shortly.

The year-old pine trees waved golden candles caught in front of a falling sun, golden tassels waving atop thin green bodies. Hundreds of grasshoppers flushed ahead of me like coveys of miniature quail. The wings of a red-tailed hawk skulled the wind. Quail whistled in the folds of Dead Man's field. Turkeys hobnobbed through the hardwoods. Spring is for dreaming, fall for killing.

That night, the moonlight was suddenly fractured by clouds; a light more venerable than the sun's. Its elfish glow bathed the fields ahead of the storm advancing from the west. Rain came like a migration of gray birds. Thunder shook the windows, which hummed; the bed moved a little. I remembered a girl who carried a flying squirrel in her pocket to school. In the morning there were thousands of frogs, frogs everywhere: tree frogs, cricket frogs, chorus frogs, squirrel frogs, barking frogs, gopher frogs. I pulled an oak toad out of the swimming pool, observed the pulsating innards of a miniature green frog through the windowpane, drove over flat frogs on the blacktop. There were bullfrogs in the toilet bowls, the shower, the sink, anywhere it was damp. This was the year of the frog.

Baby wood ducks free-fell into the pond and swam away. Crows bathed and cawed. The pond became a parking lot. Steam rose from the swamps in sheets. Sap rose by bucketfuls into the trees, whose tops woke every morning misty with fog. Through the coppery sounds of darkness I heard the screams of a nighthawk, the screams of a woman, the screams of dementia.

"For whom are those snakes that whistle on your heads?" cried the poet.

Flocks of white cattle egrets *(Bubulcus ibis)* visit us in the spring and summer, clouds of thin birds with long, yellow bills and darting, black eyes, clouds that break up and fall to earth like white pillowcases, modest in stature but predators who know their business. They hunt the fields for insects and mice, stalk the wet-weather ponds, gorge on tadpoles and lizards, run after the tractor bobbing their heads like apples in water, trill their throat feathers, dismember their prey, kill, fight off the competition, and, when crowded, swallow living things. While plowing one spring I separated a quail from her brood. The fledglings, hardly larger than bumblebees, scurried into the tall grass while their mother drew me away, stumbling here and there in front of the tractor, dropping her wings, pulling her vision of danger farther and farther from her young; behind me the cattle birds fanned out; the baby quail squealed until one by one they were discovered, and then there were none. Bill carries his revolver on the tractor and in the spring shoots at white birds; years later, the flocks recognize the farm, the tractor, and the sting of ratshot, and don't drop in as often.

Red beacons advertise the arrival of a hundred or more red-winged blackbirds into the pale green branches of the water oak next to my bird feeder. Aggressive inside their weight class, red-wings live on the muscle, and in each other's faces, bullying all potential competition except the Brewer's blackbird, an evil-looking bit of business mantled in purple with a long triangular beak and a disposition for eating lizards. Brewer's blackbirds stare at the sun through custard-colored eyes, expecting trouble from every cloud. Down the line and far too timid to claim a piece of the feeder is the northern cardinal, an attentive gentleman who usually invites his mate along. At the bottom of the pecking order lives the bland-looking field sparrow, who has nothing to say about anything.

We all crouch at passing shadows, but birds look good doing it; stylized renditions of Audubon eyes. Predation from above still lives in the memory of man. A merlin once took position for a while in a dead tree near the feeder, harassing the songbirds more by its immobility than its infrequent stoops. I saw it hit a robin, who got away with a collar of featherless pink skin as a reminder of their meeting. The merlin chased a red-winged blackbird into the window in front of my desk, startling me and breaking the blackbird's head. The blackbird didn't die but recuperated under the building, returning to the feeder daily for weeks, bald-headed and cross-beaked from the impact, looking like a particularly odd version of scissors' hands.

On a blustery June evening brilliant with white clouds and sun, I flushed a single bobwhite quail from under a planted pine tree, a tree as tall and delicate as a young girl. High in the sky the wind blew with a warm ferocity, and from the branches of a solitary oak a Cooper's hawk rose from her nest and met the quail head-on. Feathers streamed back to me, soft, lovely feathers unendurably light on the wind.

All the dark birds but one
rush from the river
leaving only the stillness of their language
—Yaqui Indian

Summer

I

B obwhite quail are small, succulent, and randy, the hen a tender morsel of femininity with a heart rate so high that warmly nestled in my hand the bird conjures the bewitching memory of a young girl's breast.

Someone once said, "A hen is merely the egg's way of making another egg." The book says that in terms of quail family-planning, the time span from romance to hatching is roughly fifty days: ten days for courting and building a nest, seventeen days for laying, and twenty-three for incubating.

In April the birds mate, the grass looks blue, the corn casts short shadows, and the blooming dogwoods underline the temporary fragility of the spring forest. Two months later, when the hatchlings abandon the warm, liquid safety of their

eggs, the heat is that of a boiler room, the underbrush burst-
ing, and the earth swollen from passing rains. The smell of a
Southern summer benumbs me in its lustfulness. Rising from
the forest floor like colorless fog, it exhales the lascivious
breath of all the women I've ever dreamed of possessing.

The incubating duties of bobwhite quail do not rest
altogether on the maternal instincts of the hens; the males,
like their modern human counterparts, get involved. The hub
of the couple's world for almost two months is the nest,
which remains unattended until the hen has finished laying an
average of fourteen eggs at a rate of one a day. If the nest is
destroyed the couple starts over, but the clutch grows smaller,
following a pattern of diminishing returns. The incubating
process begins when the last egg is laid, a three-week tour of
duty that involves sitting and protecting the nest as well as
turning the clutch over once a day to keep the embryos from
adhering to the egg membrane. Eggs discharge carbon di-
oxide, which is not conducive to healthy embryos, so by
nudging them the hens also circulate air through the nest.
The nest is left untended during the couple's meals. Berries
are favored at that time of year for their availability and high
sugar content. If the hen is killed, or for any reason abandons
the nest—which happens often, particularly early on in the
incubation—the male takes over the sitting chores and later
the education of the hatchlings.

There have been insinuations of adultery among
quail, a thought that pleases me a great deal, and one that
telemetry—the application and monitoring of a small radio
transmitter attached to a subject, in this case quail—will soon
prove one way or the other. What we do know is that the

species is basically family-oriented, possessing fierce protective qualities and good staying power. Percentage-wise, very few broods result from the couple's first nesting endeavors. Incubating is a dangerous business, and predation, weather, farming, and the poor managerial practices of first-time parents affect the outcome, but because bobwhites are genetically forewarned of failure, they are also genetically programmed to renest two or three times a summer to ensure the survival of the species. These nesting failures, incurred early in the season, account for prime hatching time being late July instead of early June, if one counts backward to the whistlings of March.

For three weeks before entering the world, the embryo grows inside the inseminated egg, breathing the gases exchanged between the shell and the egg's soft inner lining, twitching inside its cocoon, growing wings and feet and an oversized head. Hours before hatching the embryo deliberately moves its beak within striking distance of the shell and pierces the protective membrane, gaining access to its first gulp of oxygen; soon after it jerks backward, and the beak—more specifically a small tool known as an egg tooth—rips through the shell in the process called piping. With an unlimited quantity of oxygen now available the hatchling begins a counter-clockwise trip inside the egg, splitting the shell and emerging as a soggy, down-covered bobwhite quail. The process of birth lasts a matter of hours and is well choreographed in that a chorus of "clicking" sounds from inside each individual egg during the final hours of the embryo's imprisonment alerts the rest of the clutch that birth is imminent. It is a program that prompts a basketful of one-ounce bobwhites to hatch simultaneously. As soon as the natal down is dry, the parents lead their brood away from the obsolete and dangerous nest into a world of equal unkindnesses.

Jim Buckner's feelings on early hatches of bobwhite quail are pretty radical. "If I had my druthers, I'd step on every nest I could find, until the first of July." The reasoning behind these heretical words is that the earlier quail hatch, the longer they are exposed to weather and predation. Mammalian predation intensifies during the summer months, as do the number and diversity of prey. Summer weather is intense and critical to the survival of the fledglings. Rain, hail, and floods account for most of the 50-percent mortality that occurs in quaildom during the first fortnight of life. The birds have the resilience of the rural poor: destroy their home and they build a new one. Therefore, in terms of survival, even though the later nest would contain fewer eggs, if those eggs hatched in September rather than June or July, the clutch would be exposed to less weather and less predation.

I visualized Jim scrambling quail eggs for the welfare of the population and asked him how his theory was received by the old-guard plantation owners who live and die by what is referred to locally as the "Thomasville tradition."

"I don't mention it," he said without a smile.

All too familiar with the mind-set of the wealthy, I said, "Tradition is the excuse of small imaginations."

II

The black-and-orange monarch butterflies that float over the farm on powdery wings land on the scats of predators and, given the chance, cannibalize each other. Ruby-throated hummingbirds dart tongues as long as their bodies into the heart of carmine-colored columbines and, using their bills as foils, fence over the sugar water in the feeders. Bumblebees swarm the tiny violet flowers that cloak the bicolor Lespedeza shrubs, and white-tailed fawns fall out of their mothers onto the soft grassy arbors of summer. On a morning walk, my English pointer followed her nose into a thicket and ran back out, yodeling and queer-eyed, her tail between her legs, closely followed by the high-stepping hooves of a white-tailed doe. The doe would have killed

Mabel had she caught her, but she didn't, and the element of danger enhanced the comic moment of her escape.

An immature, sharp-shinned tiercel took to eating mole crickets off the lawn in the late afternoon when no one was watching but me. The little hawk, invisible until it opened its wings, studied the earth from inside the branches of a live oak and swooped at the only piece of unstable turf in an otherwise orderly expanse of greenery. The raptor landed talons first, crushing the dirt tunnel, ripping into the ground with its beak, dragging the two-inch-long insect out of the earth. The accipiter stood on the grass for a while, savoring the taste. I equate the first doves of the year with large grains of sturgeon roe. The sharp-shinned must have similar thoughts about mole crickets because the choice of meals on the farm is plentiful.

In the last decade, a joint invasion of armadillos from the south and coyotes from the west settled into northern Florida. Armadillos sleep an average of nineteen hours a day and wake up with either grubs or worms on their minds, which brings them to my garden at night in times of drought. In the morning a child's shoe would fit in the spade-shaped holes under the sprinklers where their favorite food rose to moisture. Armadillos are too simple-minded to run away from a light and too stubborn to be discouraged, except by death, and they take an incredible amount of killing. I once shot an armadillo through the head with a .38-caliber Magnum at two o'clock in the morning and watched it perform bloody somersaults on my porch for ten minutes before lying down. Another time, although mortally wounded, a large male armadillo ran between my houseguest's legs, ricocheted off his Labrador, and fell into the swimming pool, feet churning, body sinking, and blood trailing the advertisement of its descent to the bottom, where it came to rest upside down. Not an attractive sight for two friends who had just finished pontificating on the ethics of killing. Our dogs peered into the pool, and so did we, caught between the horror of the rising plume of armadillo blood and a classic bit of old-time comedy. Jim Fergus looked at me in the yellow glow of the outside lights and remarked, thin-lipped, "What do you think the animal-rights people would have to say about this bit of ignominy?"

Chaos drifted through the ranks of the golf club a few summers back when my playing partner and I were the first to stumble upon the remains of a newborn fawn in the middle of the fairway of the par-three third hole. Our footprints in the dew led the players that followed us to where the coyote had munched on the deer's posterior. The women members putted in tears and their husbands volunteered to form a posse.

I don't own or like sheep (for the same reasons I don't like cows), but if I did own sheep I'm sure I would shoot coyotes. They do take deer and turkey and a quail or two off the farm every year, but that's not reason enough for me to kill them. My livelihood does not depend on the survival of my game. I raise wild things for the pleasure of raising wild things, and if they are eaten by other wild things, so be it. I am much more inclined to kill a stray dog or cat than a wild predator, and as for the armadillos, I guess my relationship with them is one of *bonne guerre*. If I catch one tearing up the place I'll shoot it.

The truth is that I like coyotes. I like their family tree,

their cunning, and their adaptability to a habitat that was foreign to them a century ago; but mostly I like to hear them at
night, when the high notes of their lupine melodies scale the
vertebrae of my neck. Now that the coyote has moved into
the Southeastern states and has replaced the almost extinct
panther and the endangered fox, it is seen, in the minds of
some, as a new and formidable threat to wildlife.

Then there are the E.A.s (Fred Turner, in his book *A
Border of Blue,* defines E.A.s as Educated Assholes), who feel
that the coyote doesn't belong east of the Mississippi. As if
Argentinian Bahai grass belongs in Florida, or hyacinths or
melaleuca or any of a thousand other species we shortsight-
edly introduced to the country. It is as it is because we
changed the rules—we killed off the bears, the cats, and the
wolves—and the coyote has moved into a biological slot to
replace them, to keep under a semblance of control the cotton rats, the opossums, the raccoons, the snakes and . . . the
list goes on. The bottom line is that the coyote has as much
right to pursue game as does the eagle, the alligator, the blue
jay, and the armadillo. The biologist J. B. S. Haldane said,
"Civilization is based not only on men, but on plants and
animals." Our behavior in respect to our fellow humans differs from our behavior toward animals only in terms of numbers and the fear of reprisal. So far there have been more
animals to mistreat than humans, but as our own population
reaches saturation, the situation will even itself out.

If one is raising turkey, sheep, ostrich, or llamas for
profit, coyotes should probably be dealt with. Some farmers
inject antifreeze into hot dogs and toss them into the woods.
Antifreeze kills slowly by boring holes in the stomach lining.
Local farmers bait meat with pesticides. The use of poison is

economical, even if it is cowardly, and justifies the outrage of those who are opposed to killing, but then who am I to tell another man what is right and wrong? I shoot armadillos for rooting up daylilies but protect coyotes because their songs make me happy. Civilized behavior functions within the parameters of the soul, an intangible innocence that defines us as human beings. The soul is the domain of love, of God, of art, nature, music, children, parents; the forgotten domains, trampled of late under the hooves of our ever-multiplying herd.

Every predator in the world would like to eat a bob-white quail. Some don't, for reasons of the bird's celerity, but those that are shrewd enough and have the speed will continue to pursue the fat little bird until the end of time. Among those are: opossums, raccoons, skunks, weasels, cotton rats, foxes, dogs, cats, crows, blue jays, cattle egrets, chickens, turkeys, and red ants. Also, snakes: coach and whip and king and black; sharp-shinned and Cooper's hawks, shrikes, parasites, and me. Hawks attack from above, snakes from below. Long-billed birds take aim at its brain, and fire ants infiltrate pipped eggs and devour the embryos before they are born. Summer rains flood its nest, and droughts wrinkle the egg membranes like old snakeskins so that the chicks can't pip their way out and thus suffocate. The list is incomplete but does hint of mayhem.

We humans raise quail, release quail, protect them, feed them, shoot them, hang them, pluck them, cook them, and serve them to our very best friends. The bobwhite quail is one of the most sought-after items in nature's deli, which may explain the fact that they are scarce, paranoid, and run like hell.

III

June 25, 1992
Noon, 96° Fahrenheit

Fish crows turn to face the smallest breath of air with open beaks. Half a dozen bobwhite quail whistle. The light is white. So is the surface of the pond, disturbed by riffle beetles skating over its milky surface in long reaches that end abruptly in dimples. The heat is such that I see through cataract eyes, heat rising out of the earth, a condition that will last three months and that more than once will scare me into believing the land is on fire.

Anhingas break the surface of the lake with brims as wide as my hand sideways in their beaks. Anhingas hunt underwater alongside the turtles and alligators; at water-level they swim like snakes. I watch them waddle up on stumps, smack brim against logs and throw them in the air to make them fall headfirst down their throats. Then they open their wings wide to dry. Yellow light highlights their primary feathers and long, pale, buff-colored necks, which flop back and forth from the bird's chest to its back, to each wing and back again, slowly, languorously. In flight the anhinga's head is almost invisible, an extension of a neck ending in a sharp, thin, yellow bill, fashioned long before man invented the spear. In the water, the narrow head never stops moving, swimming, angling, looking back and front—a distant cousin of the Loch Ness Monster. Steam rises out of the pond.

My farmer friend gave me four geese, two brown ones and two white. I wanted a pair of Canadas, but that's what I got. The brown geese have orange-rimmed eyes; the white geese have yellow rims and blue eyes. They all have orange bills and wrinkled legs with thick nails filed to a point, and their stomachs are shaped like a woman's purse. On hot days like today they lie around and nod.

"The trout won't bite when the cows are lying down," Bill tells my doctor friend this morning. He and another doctor had been casting flies at bass since dawn. "Check Channel Six, at five-fifty-five P.M., Doc; they broadcast the Solunar Tables. Feeding time's the same for fish and cows. It's too hot. The cows were already on the ground when I drove up this morning."

Doc tells Bill about the cottonmouth they saw swimming high in the water shortly after sunup. Bill spits out his plug and says, "I was fishing this hole one time when I saw this cottonmouth moccasin swallering her young ones. I shot her in the belly, and damn if them little ones didn't spill outta her and swim away."

The doctors leave. Purple martins skim the water on the pond; some pitch in the water headfirst. Bill looks at his notebook: "I pushed up two hundred tree stumps this winter, and killed twenty-six Bell Boys (rattlesnakes). One snake about every ten stumps." He thumbs through the pages on which he records things like that, along with planting dates, maintenance dates, weather-pattern dates, the-number-of-fish-caught dates, odds-and-ends dates, etc.; a well-kept record of his year on the farm that adds weight and credibility to both our lives.

He continues, "To that, add seven moccasins and the five-foot alligator that ate the gosling. You cooked it up in butter and garlic with black beans and rice and said it didn't taste like anything." Bill keeps good records.

I listen to other figures that have to do with the price of grain and seeds while I wonder again about the ethics behind killing species that out of fear, surprise, or plain hunger could kill one of my dogs. I know, of course, that in a year's time twenty-six rattlesnakes eat hundreds of rats, and that alligators eat just as many turtles, who in turn eat just as many fish. But no matter how much I think about it, in the end, the safety of the dogs, like the safety of children, prevails. It has something to do with the humanization of pets.

I shot a yellow-bellied slider the first year I was here because I was told that there were too many turtles and they would eat all the brim. When the turtle blew up, I wondered what possessed me to do such a stupid thing and for a while I lost my mind. Perhaps it is a sign of abnormal times or simply a sign that my time is coming, but in either case, every year it is getting more difficult to kill. I need help in the matter, help from my dogs who so love to hunt the birds I so love to eat. In cases like this, I pray for fall to come quickly, before I forget how much I love to hunt, how maudlin I can get when I drink red wine, and that, on the average, quail live less than a year.

IV

Charley Johnson is an independent contractor who worked heavy machinery for the previous owner of the farm. Since the beginning of my tenure he has built two dams, knocked over hundreds of worthless trees, pushed fire lanes, dug ditches, broken down, ran his crawler into mud holes and out of gas, pissed me off, and made me laugh. Charley is also part-owner of a raw bar in Cairo, Georgia, and cooks a pretty good barbecue. When I give a party we serve his oysters and my pigs. So far no one has died or complained.

In the 1960s Charley worked construction on one end of Grand Bahama Island while I fished on the other. I understand Bahamian time so I understand Charley, and it amuses me that someone I met thirty years after the fact is keeping up the old island tradition of resting from taking a nap.

I, too, cherish my naps, and I daydream, and I still drink rum, so when Charley doesn't show up for a week it rings a bell. Being a sucker for memories I usually forgive Charley, and to be honest I'm not sure how I'd behave if our situations were reversed.

He is an operator-owner, and despite the fact that the owner in him is still living in the islands (a stronghold for zero maintenance), the operator in him has seen it all, including the death of fellow operators. He owns more nonfunctional pieces of equipment than functional ones, but like a gunslinger he travels with his favorites: Gerty, the excavator, and baby Gert, the small bulldozer that moves sideways like a land crab. Both machines are painted commercial yellow and oil black, and have to be started with a screwdriver. Big Gerty finally "passed" (as they say down here) a while back, after sixteen years of service, but little Gert is still with us and pushing dirt as I write. The smoke and ooze that used to leak out of big Gerty would have given any state official an apoplectic fit, but for reasons I will make clearer, I do my best to keep the government off my land.

Charley's usually smiling face turns copper brown by June and he advertises the pleasant fifty-year-old belly of a man who enjoys an evening splash. His grandmother was a full-blood Creek, a lineage I would be proud of, but given that very little has been written about the Southeastern Indians, Charley's reticence to talk about his family tree is understandable. In any case, who wants to relive century-old atrocities, atrocities that are no better or worse than those committed today.

The Creek laws of marriage did not allow a man from a high rank or blood to marry a woman of the same social class, only a woman from a lower caste. This was implemented to obviate inbreeding and keep things in perspective. Take it from a genuine blue blood and sometime dog-breeder: the Creek law beats the hell out of line breeding.

Charley and Bill are as different in their approach to work as two men can be, and yet they are both bound by the pull of the earth.

The ten-acre pond I inherited with the farm had been built in the fifties and, as far as ponds go, it was a good one, with a number of big bass and brim, catfish and shiners, crawfish and turtles. The problem was that no one had fished it in years and most of the bass were stunted from being restricted to a small area, like fish in an overcrowded aquarium. One solution was to catch and keep all the small bass with old, odd-looking skulls, but more tempting was to make the pond bigger. We did both. Bill caught 673 fish and I studied the possibility of raising the existing dam by nine feet, which would throw water over twenty additional acres of land, turning a puddle into a measurable piece of water.

For days Bill and Charley and I "shot" the basins with a surveyor's transit to determine how high the water would rise. We walked through bulrushes, pond weeds, thornbushes, and over decayed tree trunks, calling out numbers glimpsed through a monolense, planting flags and side-stepping snakes. We flagged the perimeter of the lake and studied the value of the trees that would have to be timbered, the cost of moving the dirt, the fuel to propel the machinery, the yards of cement, the PVC pipes, the couplings, and, when it was all said and laid out, I was left with a choice: to apply for permits or not.

The water would fill a hardwood bottom that I wanted to clear-cut before raising the dam. Florida law requires a permit to build a dam and another one to touch anything resembling a swamp. The permit to raise the existing foundation would have to come from the Northwest Florida Water Management District, an agency of the state that regulates the use of every single drop of water in its jurisdiction, right down to the laying of a drainpipe on private property. The permit to clear-cut the hardwoods would have to come from the Soil Conservation Bureau, but because there were springs in the bottom and a certain amount of backed-up water, it was going to be a tough permit to obtain for ecological reasons.

The fact that I would alter one ecosystem for another, trade five acres of swamp for thirty acres of water (which would result in the same amount of shoreline swamp), that I would gain as well as lose species in the process, that if anything I was adding life instead of draining it was not going to matter. Government agencies, in which science and bureaucracy compete in an unholy marriage of rules and arrogance, are not receptive to common sense. I abide by the law most of the time but draw the line when I'm ordered to do something I feel is corrupt or stupid. Life is too short. The choice was simple: Screw the permits.

Two days later, three cars, two flatbed trucks, and seven men with a dozen handheld saws of varied length and weight pulled into the farm. The timber crew—no more legal than I was—brought along water, food, girlie magazines for the lunch breaks, toilet paper for the obvious, and a short, squat, tree-stalking machine called a clipper that looked like an upside-down hockey net made of steel. It was a frightening demon on huge rubber tires, swinging an obscene steel trunk with band saws incorporated into its circular claw, which clamped around the base of trees and, while the machine hugged the trunk, sawed through the tree's heart with its teeth. A very strange and efficient piece of steel I have since run from in my dreams.

The trucks piled with hardwoods rolled from the farm to the Georgia border for a solid week, leaving behind what all timber crews leave behind: treetops, dangling bark, jagged stumps, gutted earth, human dung, pop cans, desolation, and the tangible proof of a dead woodlot. I have done business with lumber companies on two continents and have yet to deal with one that has the integrity of an insurance company. They differ only in the species they gouge, which in this case was my hardwoods. I cashed a small check and prayed I hadn't made a big mistake.

Charley moved the Gert sisters into position, and for the next four months I watched more dirt being moved than I had ever seen moved in my life. When it was time I rented a pan, and timed it going back and forth over the five-hundred-foot dam, shaving off a thin skin of clay from one shoulder of the slope, dropping it on the dam, shearing off a second slice on the other slope, and back again. The dam ate fifteen thousand cubic feet of red dirt at the rate of thirteen cubic yards every six minutes. Talk about a yawn.

Red dust followed the machinery on dry days and red clay squirted up between our toes on wet ones. On those days little Gert expressed a desire to slip sideways into the pond, so every time it rained for half an hour, work stopped for the day. Conversations centered themselves with bottomless stupidity on the weather. Eventually I gave up blaming God and took to drinking early on rainy days. We also talked about denunciations and fines and, like birds, kept our eyes cocked at the sky for danger in the shape of spotter planes.

The mountain of clay grew slowly, gradually, one inch at a time, until one day and a thousand mishaps later the new dam towered over the original pond, 15 feet wide at the top, 90 at the base, and 535 feet long. As a precaution against rainstorms and erosion we seeded the mastodon with grass, covered it with hay, and dressed it in sheets of old sunbleached muslin, remnants of the shade-tobacco days.

Eighteen Months Later

The house I use as an office sits on the water's edge, at the juncture of the old pond and the one we raised out of the swamp. I am waiting for the water to fill up the pond for the second time, and as it does it feels like the bottom of the world is rising up to meet me. Last year the pond filled up in one month, the wettest January in memory. It was a beautiful sight, particularly as the water stopped rising exactly where we had planted the high-water flags, half a year earlier.

But in March a small leak sprung on the far side of the water-logged edifice where an original culvert had been poorly cemented, and although the leak was little more than a stain on the clay, when it began to grow it reminded me of stitches snapping on a wound. The fact of the matter is that we screwed up. To save a few hundred dollars I chose to pour cement on the existing pipe instead of having Gerty dig and pull it out of the dam. As it turned out, penny-wise and pound foolish.

A week later the rains came again, hard, and at eleven o'clock on a Saturday night the wet spot suddenly delaminated. Bill called: "If we don't cut her now, she'll be gone by morning."

Gerty shook and belched under the lights, her steel claw digging in, loosening the packed clay and forking it into her bucket with the same cantankerous tenacity she had exhibited the summer before. A portable generator threw light on the advancing waters and the deepening chasm and backlit a thin jet of silvery hydraulic fluid that squirted out of one of Gerty's sunburned hoses when she strained. At four in the morning the pond squeezed itself through a ten-foot-wide opening and tore into the swamp with irrepressible finality.

Twenty hours later the beautiful expanse of dark water that Charley created was down to its original depth. I was back to square one, with a leak to fix and the Northwest Florida Water Management District on my back. The spillage had run half a mile down a dense, hardwood creek bottom before crossing the county blacktop road under a cement bridge. The clay-colored water escaped into my neighbor's woods and headed for the Oklockonee River, already disfigured from a saturated water table. The Water Management Office, informed of an unnatural discharge, followed the

muddy water back to its source and officially stopped the repairs; not for raising the dam by nine feet—something they
either didn't know about or chose not to pursue—but for
liberating the pond without their permission. The fact that we
cut the dam during a storm, in the middle of the night on a
weekend, was neither here nor there.

The structure would have to be rebuilt according to
modern specs, which meant four-to-one slopes, yards of cement and steel sunk into the trouble area, a drain system, a
ninety-foot spillway, months of waiting for permits, adminis-
trative costs, surveys, judgments, engineers imposed by the
government, fines, and decrees. The circle was completed
when, tens of thousands of dollars later, I asked what the official orders would have been had I reached someone by phone
in the middle of that rainy Florida night. The answer was
"Just what you did."

Having spent eleven years in boarding school I react
poorly to orders, but as I hadn't asked for a permit to raise the
dam—much less queried the environmental agency about
clear-cutting the swamp—I tiptoed through the bureaucratic
china store by shutting up and eating six months of crow.

V

The green smell of July in Tallahassee serves as a reminder to those in wildlife management that green smells aren't finite and that the end of the planting season for bobwhites (and every other grain-eating species) is at hand. Crops such as corn and Egyptian wheat are already in the ground and in normal years will produce hard seeds through the first half of January; in wet years that same grain will sour before Christmas. The longest-lasting and most reliable crop I use is Sorghum NK 300 (another nonnative plant shipped from Africa), planted the second week of July—about as late as we dare stretch it in northern Florida without running into an early freeze. We plant long strips (two hundred by fifteen feet) next to the plum trees and parallel to the planted pines and bicolored Lespedeza, offering an intense diversity of cover, food, and edges according to the formula of food adjoining escape cover equals minimum exposure to predation. The worst thing I can do for my tenants is to grow small, isolated food plots, which will in no time be known as accipiter corner, a quail-McNugget repository for raptors, a death row for bobwhite quail. Bill throws an occasional ninety-degree turn in the food patches and plants in long, lazy curves, which mathematically promote edges. It takes eight pounds of sorghum per plot, which we fertilize two weeks later and let the sun do the rest.

It was common a few years ago to partially cut the trunk of oak trees until they lay on the ground, leaving a section of the trunk connected so that the sap would keep flowing to the leaves. The quail felt safe under the fallen branches and the hawks used the nearest tree as a stooping scaffold. In France I once watched a bustard visit a covey of eleven gray partridge in a twenty-acre alfalfa field every afternoon. Two weeks later it had eaten every single bird. I don't doubt that, given the same particulars, a Cooper would emulate his European cousin.

Bobwhite quail eat as many as fifty thousand insects a year, reason enough to sow brown-top millet, which attracts all the bugs a quail could wish for. However, as brown-top is expensive, and because the natural propagation of life and natural food in the Southeast is so rich in the summer and fall, I don't use millet as extensively as some with deeper pockets. Also, when the fledgling bald eagles scream down from inside their nests at my bird dogs and the frost and rain have beaten the life out of the natural food and cover—in other words, when help is really needed—the brown-top has long since passed.

The actual numbers of food plots and additional cover can be broken down into a series of equations that take into account the resolve of the owner and the weight of his wallet. I plant forty strips of sorghum, half a dozen one-acre cornfields, two big cornfields used as dove fields, and three one-acre plots in the woods, on which I experiment with either Kobe Lespedeza or Egyptian wheat and this year buckwheat—I would like to find a grain with which to replace corn, but so far haven't found one.

The list of commercial quail food is long and keeps growing longer every year. Most of it is designer bird food. Expensive and wasteful, the motto of our time. Corn, sorghum, soybeans, and brown-top millet can handle 90 percent of any additional food needs a bobwhite could have. I go overboard on food because I like food, and because I am a glutton I feed tens of thousands of nongame birds with the vigor I feed my human friends. Last year my quail were so fat they self-basted under the duress of applied heat.

One day I will try alternating crops, such as planting winter wheat, Egyptian wheat, and buckwheat all in the same year, as sort of a wheat festival. My ultimate objective is to abandon all annual crops and rely on the perennial plants such as partridge peas, protective cover that has already been planted, rotation burns, and extensive spring disking to carry a natural quail population. I am interested to see how the birds will react and what it will do to the population. But for now I enjoy watching the corn and sorghum dry and grow old and tawny in time with the broom sedge and gum trees. A matter of taste.

VI

By the end of August there is something frantic about the unanswered calls of the bobwhite quail. What was meant to be a season of promise and glory has slowly disintegrated into a jeremiad, an admission of failure. Indecent bachelor whistles have become mournful wails, acknowledging among other things an imminent shrinking of gonads. If I shoot that bird next winter it will not be as flavorful as the quail that has known the spasms of ecstasy. At the very least, rapture darkens the heart. Therefore, following one bit of idiotic insight with another, I might as well explain the Mexican quail controversy.

Almost everywhere in the South exist swamp quail, birds that have adapted to gloomier surroundings and are darker in plumage for living in such places. Because dark objects look smaller than light ones, and because swamp birds always fly back to the safety of darkness, they appear smaller and seem to fly faster than their peers living on higher ground.

The locals refer to these little creatures as Mexican quail *(Colinus virginianus texanus),* and say things about them like, "Before they introduced them Mexicans you never saw a quail light in a tree," or, "Them Mexican quail are nothing but roadrunners. They taught our partridge bad habits." In point of fact, a deal *was* made with the Mexican government to purchase between three and four hundred thousand *texanus* quail. They were carefully distributed throughout our southern and central states, and a percentage of the imported birds survived and bred with *Colinus virginianus,* but, contrary to popular belief, the Mexican quail were paler, not darker in color than our native species, and the purchase was made between 1910 and 1930. In quail terms, sixty-plus generations ago; in human terms it would be like blaming ethnic cleansing on King Arthur's crusaders.

By August, 90 percent of the bobwhite quail on the farm are busy following their parents, pushing pinfeathers, hunting grasshoppers, and sipping dew. The remaining 20 percent are either mourning the passing of their libido or are doggedly renesting for the umpteenth time in the hopes of rearing a late brood, young ones that will bear on opening day the unattractive sobriquet of "squealers."

VII

All the red-winged blackbirds are gone to the mountains, where it's cool. The morning glory vines have shimmied every cornstalk and planted pine and fencerow on the farm, embracing without prejudice one and all, overwhelming the undercarriage of nature while flaunting strings of languorous pastel flowers. The exception to this riot of polite colors is the tiny scarlet morning glory, a tulip-shaped flower that jumps out of the weeds like a redhead at a Primitive Baptist prayer meeting.

Waterfalls of kudzu yield to gravity like a woman's hair. Someone once said that if New England is a woman's brains, the South is her belly.

Green darters, dragonflies the size of hummingbirds,

rise out of the pond and roar about, terrorizing the rest of the insect world. My friend in Alabama shoots mosquito hawks with .22-caliber ratshot. Cicadas wearing an extra layer drone through the heavy breath of summer looking for the right pine tree to grasp and shed a shell. Old-timers feed the ground shells to their coon dogs to make them better tree dogs. Pine trees hit by lightning rot in a month. Yellow butterflies huddle face-to-face in the middle of dirt roads and scatter in the air like flower petals. Bullbats (nighthawks, order of goatsuckers) dive at insects with gaping mouths; the air growls when they pull up short of the ground. The Mississippi and swallowtail kites replace the bullbats. They too swoop from tremendous heights at the locusts that flush ahead of the tractor. The grasshoppers are as big as my thumb and the kites catch them in their talons, inches from my face. When the birds have reached altitude they raise both talons to their chin and eat the grasshoppers in midair, stalling their wings in the process.

White rain rushes across the water. Raindrops the size of marbles dimple the pond. In June eleven woodies fell out of the duck box in front of my studio. There are only three left, not counting the hen. A late afternoon rain break under the toolshed in August. It rained on the first day of dog days last year and, just as the saying goes, it went on to rain for forty days. This year, however, there hasn't been a shower on the farm since June, and the sun hides behind a permanent heat haze. The clay is so hard that in places the fields have split in two. No one has seen dew on the grass in weeks.

Charley has been pushing dirt. Bill has been watering the trees—sawtooth oaks, sycamores, Lombardy poplars:

thirty-three in all—that we planted this winter. He waters by hand, out of fifty-gallon drums lashed to the trailer, and a five-gallon bucket. I promise to buy him a water wagon. He drinks coffee, nods at the rain that finished his job, and prods absentmindedly into the small round holes in the clay outside the shed with a piece of grass, to tickle the doodlebugs. He looks tired from toting all that water, but if I say so he'll deny it. Age may have pulled some weight off his frame, but in his head Bill is as strong as he was when he was twenty. The only time I ever raised my voice in the eight years I've known him was to force liquids down his throat one burning summer afternoon while he was pouring cement behind the dam. The temperature was one hundred degrees, and there was as much color in his face as there was wind at the bottom of the twenty-eight-foot structure. He obliged me because I am his boss, but he wasn't happy about it and for months afterward insisted he had been fine and was aware of his capacities. That may be, but he hasn't accepted the wearisome implications of time yet.

Charley points to a purple beetle, laughs, and slaps his leg. A hard-shelled purple turd-tumbler has reared up on its gnarled hindquarters, churning the dusty clay, pushing and herding a dog shit large enough to die under. Charley said, "Damn if that ain't a lot of tumbling."

"You're telling me."

VIII

I was introduced to hunting by a Normandy gamekeeper when I was seven years old. The gamekeeper was a huge middle-aged man who killed crippled birds with his teeth. My weapon was a single-barreled nine-millimeter shotgun. I shot a hare my first day in the field, wounded it, and cried. I was not allowed to shoot hares—rabbits *oui*, hares *non*—but I did, and hit the animal in the hindquarters. I cried because I was in trouble, because the hare was screaming and dragging itself in circles on the ground, and because I had never killed with a gun before and it scared me. My tears fell on the rough cloth of the gamekeeper's hunting coat. He made me finish what I had started but was sensitive enough not to rub blood on my face as was the custom.

It was a wonder I ever picked up another gun, but I did. The very thing that had frightened me, the conscious and formal resolution to kill and the tangible weight of that decision in my hands, pushed me out the door and into the woods two days later. Although the motives have changed, hunting began with killing. My affair with nature has since then been related to the pursuit of game. I studied a species because I wanted to kill it, and I looked at things through the quick, impatient eyes of the hunter; eyes that darted under brush piles, anticipated movement, plotted courses, assessed what belonged in the shadows and what didn't; eyes that learned to recognize the details that made me good at what I did. I looked at nature from the narrow angle necessary to act out my passion and always with defined objectives in mind. I looked at a piece of country for the game it hid. I moved differently, dressed differently, and I thought differently from 95 percent of the other hunters, but the bottom line was that I was one of them and still am. I killed a lot of birds in those days and was good at it because I had no regrets. Game was for the taking, and I was galvanized by the glory of numbers; restraint and empathy came later.

The specific mission of hunting slanted my vision of nature throughout my life, to the extent that even as I grow older and spend more time in the field without a gun I still think, look, and move as though I am hunting. A quest lives in me. I am a hunter like other people are bankers, and along with the seduction of the landscape, my dogs, the efficaciousness of some of my shooting, and the mild aura of danger that follows any hunter in the field, the stroke that killed was always at the core of the sport that took me to the field. This is a waning passion in the gene pool of mankind, now that hunting has no meaningful role in society, no survival merits, no reason to exist except as a sport. In my case it is a sport as natural as dancing or making love, and just as ancient, but to others it is an abomination, and I do understand why.

I didn't always obey the rules or the ethics of hunting and have over the years used my guns for all the wrong reasons, but when all is said and done I will make sure I have given back more than I have taken, which I presume is the essence of conservation. In the process of being comfortable with what I do for sport and how I go about it, I see much more of the natural world than most. But keeping things in perspective, I see less than a farmer, a rancher, a surveyor, and all those who are out there every day making ends meet.

As a hunter I am conscious of food and cover, space and time, predation and disease, hunger and overbreeding, and I understand the effects that these ingredients have on the species I hunt and those I don't, including our own. In terms of pure knowledge I know less than a third-year biology student.

My farm has replaced my gun, and I don't look for the same hiding places anymore; I don't compute range and angles, I don't look for feeding patterns. I look at birds that soar under the clouds, birds that eat other birds, and birds that fish with their feet (before this is over I shall be a falconer). I look at all sorts of birds, large and small, and I look at them with gentle eyes.

I have always been a walker, but before I became a landowner I walked looking at the ground and didn't raise my eyes unless I was carrying a gun. I would pretend I was thinking but in fact was letting things pass by. In cities I walked into things because they happened to be there. I lost a bet to a woman once who guessed my astrological sign because of the way I shuffled through the streets of Paris wondering where my feet were taking me. "You are a Taurus," she said, "an earth person."

"Merde!" I cursed.

I tried blaming my posture on the fact that I had been thinking about ways to get into her britches, but she shook her head and laughed like Frenchwomen do. "*Cheri,* you have a tongue. Use it next time. I might have said yes, I might have said no, but at least you would not have lost that expensive bracelet in the window." Compounding the affront, she patted me on the rear and it felt like she was burping me.

Now that I own the land I walk on, I have extended my horizons, dilated my vision, and adopted a druidlike contentment in the laws of nature. We have all reveled in the carnival of death and even lingered in the shadows of spilt blood, but those times, like the day of the great elephant herds, are gone.

There is nothing divine about man's laws; in fact they are outdated and self-serving. The laws of God and nature are just as self-serving, and because they are not remunerative they are short on compassion. Darwin once said, "Nature will tell you a direct lie if she can." So will our Congress, our children, and so will we; it is the nature of the beast.

IX

September 1, 1991

I mowed for five hours today. For two of those hours I stood on the tractor naked except for my sneakers and hat. The temperature gauge scrambled up to 120 degrees and broke. I burned my ass, swam in the pond, and went back to the house feeling tired and thirsty.

Bill and I drove the perimeters of the property that afternoon and frightened a baby fawn out of a cornfield. It ran, long-legged and awkward, in front of the car, and trembled when I carried it back to the cornfield where its mother waited. The spotted buck was all ears and hooves and knobby extremities, and its breath smelled like condensed milk.

Last year about the same time I saw a bobcat stretched out across a dirt road four feet in the air, twenty feet in front of my car. The cat sailed over the road three feet behind another fawn, this one a little older and without spots. The deer's eyes were big and black and terrified; the cat's eyes were yellow and narrow and focused. The deer turned its head when it jumped the road and there was incomprehension in its eyes. I stopped the car but didn't hear or see anything. The forest resumed its dominion over mystery.

A male bobwhite quail ran toward me, gathered speed, and flew at my legs, almost up my shorts. I counted thirteen fledglings the size of mice in the grass, running and stopping, running and stopping. The bobwhite flew across the road and pretended to fall, twisting and pulling itself upright, following the proper genetic upbringing of a drag queen.

I walked a long way around the big field at sunset. Weather helps sunsets, but there was no weather that night, just dust particles enhancing the red and purple sky my spaniel so loves to watch. At times her eyes pop out of her head for trying to take it all in. She snaps at huge grasshoppers when they fly past her head, but is happiest looking for birds.

I could barely make out the pine trees now that the weeds and vines have grown around them. In ten years, this field will turn golden in the fall and the tops of the broom sedge will gather the pale evening light, and if I am still here I will walk down a keyboard of loblolly shadows; tonight I walked past the shadows of ragweed, dog fennel, and young pine trees.

I am attracted to this field even though the trees

haven't grown up. The authority of a two-hundred-acre field. I read in Edward O. Wilson's *Biophilia* about man's natural penchant for parklike habitat, complete with hills and water and well-spaced trees. Edward O. would be pissing in high cotton if he could see this place.

At worst, a Southern summer feels like a monumental itch; at best, it is the sound of mystery, of childhood, of a string symphony tuning up, of the sounds without which the planet dies. Remove the termites from the planet and the planet will die; remove man, and except for the applause the loss will pass unnoticed.

Once or twice a week I add my own music to the big field by turning the volume up in the car's sound system and opening the doors. A boom box of size. Sometimes I replay songs that uncurl the years; usually, like my oak trees, I wave my arms and dance without moving my feet. I prefer dirty boogie, get-down, suck-an-egg kind of music; music to drink to while the dogs chase their noses. J. J. Cale and I cut quite a rug under the boughs of my trees, where there's no one but myself to criticize or tell me what to do. A man gets spoiled living like this.

A breath of gold moved into the landscape last week. Harbingers of fall, waves of partridge peas and Crotalaria moved over the landscape. I leafed through a book on Florida's wildflowers and realized that I had come upon another in a long series of disappointing educational lapses. A certain and unnerving thought came to me: I would be dead long before I knew the names of the flowers that grow on my farm.

Two white birds dance above the hardwood trees.

They are difficult to see. I think of cattle egrets because their wings are long and white. I am wrong; one is a cattle egret, the other is a mature bald eagle. It is his neck and head that are white, not his wings. An eagle dancing with an egret above the trees overlooking the pond. They are close together, slowly bending the air with their bodies, melting bodies, tango-dancing in the sky, and then they are one. The raptor holds the egret's chest in its talons. The thin, white bird hangs boneless below the eagle that flies toward a pine tree.

I move too soon. The big bird drops the cattle egret and it falls to the ground in a bundle of white feathers. The eagle lands in the pine tree and looks at me. The white bird gets up, shakes itself like a wet dog, and flies to the safety of where I stand.

Plus je vois des représentants du peuple, plus j'aime mes
chiens.

(The more I see of the people's representatives,
the more I like my dogs.)
—Comte Alfred d'Orsay, 1850

Fall

I

I cool my heels in the shade of an ironwood tree, counting doves flying into a cornfield to feed. It is clear and cold for October and the light sparkles through the auburn tassels of the cornhusks. At four-thirty in the afternoon there are 150 mourning doves on the ground, a gray wave of birds feeding on the tiny seeds of the brown-top millet that Bill sowed when he laid the corn by in June. The earth quivers and dances under the flocks of pewter-colored birds. The second phase of the dove season opens in three weeks. I am only here to listen and watch.

We planted the ten-acre field last spring and at harvesttime we left long rows of standing corn, six stalks wide, for the shooters to hide in, rows that I will mow down as the seasons progress to provide legal food. Later in the month I'll spread wheat or, if I can buy them cheaply, sunflower seeds. The day before shooting the field I'll harrow it. Technically that is baiting. The federal law decrees that the seeds must be turned under ten days prior to shooting a dove field. The state gamekeepers don't enforce that law. Historically the federal and state bodies that regulate the laws pertaining to nature don't get along. To that basic mistrust one adds the appointed game commissions composed of non-professionals and the pot boils with political intrigue, not to mention imbecility.

I believe that supplemental food is beneficial to all game and, in the case of dove fields or duck ponds, that growing it should be encouraged rather than forbidden. With more food available, the concentration of migratory birds on the land whose owners are willing to break the law would be lessened, more people would enjoy better hunting, and tens of thousands of nongame as well as game species would benefit from these legal soup kitchens. Enforcement should not be aimed at the sowing of food but at encroachments on limits. Make it tough, make it five hundred dollars for each bird over the limit, and see what happens. No one is going to mess with those numbers.

On the ground, doves look like bathroom fixtures; in the air they look like small fighter planes. A red-tailed hawk steals over the field. His broad, round wings influence the doves, who jump off the ground in a creaky clatter of gray wings. They split into groups of twenty, scatter, and rise like fireworks above the hawk who, oblivious to their concerns, glides downwind, his chestnut-colored tail spread against the breeze, his attention focused on rats and snakes and other such delicacies. The doves bank over the wet-weather pond and turn back to the millet, dipping and twisting and exposing to the falling sun a wash of pink breasts. The air is alive with glancing wings.

Dove shooting—our version of lawn shooting—is a social affair, and while the birds deserve high grades for the gunning difficulties they provide as well as for their culinary value, dove shoots fluctuate from boring to out of control. Given adequate wind and enough trees, doves make some of the best targets and, except for passing snipe, the smallest legal ones. A hot sun and a lack of birds is boring; a legal, twelve-bird limit is plenty; a barn burner is a shoot the law hopes to invite itself to; and a sneaker shoot is a barn burner the law is expected to raid and the participants to run from. I have been on every kind of dove shoot over the years and I find it amusing that nowadays, while I am perfectly happy to sit for hours with a pair of binoculars around my neck and not see what I set out to see, sitting with a gun in a dove field with no birds bores me to tears. I would like to think that my impatience stems from an ancestral urge to produce the bacon but suspect that while the act of hunting necessitates a denouement of sorts, the act of observing demands nothing more than one's eyes and the ability to muse.

I think of plucked doves glistening with butter and imagine rolling them on a hot grill while the real ones settle back down into the millet. At five-thirty an immense covey of bobwhite quail twenty-five birds strong flies out of the woods. They cast an irregular shadow over the field of black-eyed Susans that leads to the feeding doves. The quail flare in a heartbeat of wings into the first row of standing corn. Birds of all ages fill the covey, giving the assembly an odd, unraveled look. The phenomenon of these huge fall assemblies is nature's strategy for stirring the blood. These social gatherings eventually break into companies of twelve to fifteen birds that remain loosely together until spring.

The quail spread in the corn rows, feeding leisurely out of sight. The sun sets through an excess of hanging moss, an orange sun falling through gray-green living moss, decadent and ugly in its beauty. I lean against the ironwood and wait for the quail to finish eating. After a while I feel myself slowly sinking into the tree, all the way into its heart, where I feel the sap pull me underground into the unconsciousness of sleep. A cold breeze out of the north wakes me. The doves and the quail have gone; the purple light introduces a notion of winter and the harvest of wild things.

II

My neighbor, Marine Sergeant Retired B. J. Pruit, owns seven acres of land adjoining mine, on which he lives in a single-wide trailer raised on cement blocks. B.J. is in his late fifties, short, and, except for a big mouth and a perfectly round stomach, bone thin. He builds and repairs rifles and demands that the utility people, the mail lady, and the UPS delivery boys call him Sergeant.

B.J. is a martinet and a bore who will tell you that during his tenure in the corps he made life hell for his subordinates. "Rubbed some grit into the bastards, made 'em into men." I don't believe the man has the sense to pour piss out of a boot, but he does have opinions, particularly about guns and politics. His companion, Pigskin, is a mixed-breed bulldog-

Rottweiler; Pruit is most proud of him for learning to attack trees on command. Pigskin takes his job seriously, and the trees surrounding B.J.'s trailer are wanting for bark.

I went bird hunting once with B.J. and his buddy Johnny (Bubba) West on a piece of land that they leased for deer hunting but on which they swore to me there were quail. I was new in the county, accommodating because B.J. was my neighbor, and interested because I had heard he was an oddball. I should have known better, but didn't, so I got stuck riding around in Bubba's Jeep Renegade for two hours, drinking beer, dodging chew tobacco spit, and listening to the kind of trash that fuels civil uprisings.

I sat in the back seat next to Duke, a big white pointer with warts on his head. Duke was a nice old dog with some hound blood hidden in his ancestry. Every so often he would stand up and bay for no apparent reason. I could tell that Bubba liked the old dog because every time it stood up, he would reach a thick arm behind the seat and absentmindedly play with Duke's nuts, which dangled inches from my face.

B.J. spent the morning making endearing comments that ranged from a simpering "Well, no one left any buffaloes for me," to a rebellious "I want to be remembered as the man who kills the last grizzly." When I mentioned coyotes, Bubba roared, "Sums of bitches eat all my deer, bucks and butt-aids alike, don't make no difference." Butt-heads is a colloquial, low-rent nickname for does. I don't see B.J. much anymore except late in the season, when he's desperate enough to try and talk Bill out of a doe permit. I do hear him sighting in his rifles, though.

III

The morning glories, which for weeks had dressed the young pine trees in white and lavender gowns, have begun to wilt. Cold nights drag the green from their leaves. The heavy underbrush sighs and looks forward to a rest.

All but a handful of the bobwhite broods are fledged, and the young quail have sprouted grown-up feathers. Their flight is erratic, but at least they are airborne and, if vigilant, will distance themselves from most predators. A murder of crows lands on the farm during the corn harvest, hundreds of cheeky black birds alighting on the branches of dead trees, fighting among themselves, chasing jays and woodpeckers, mocking hawks, plucking worms from behind the harrow's job, and taunting each other like the children they are. Here and there, pink-and-white butterflies dapple aimlessly over the dying grass and once in a while a grasshopper lands weakly on my shirt. For the first time in eight months I think of quail as food and surprise myself by aiming my finger at passing doves. The year always starts for me in the fall, possibly because I spent a long decade in boarding school, but probably because September introduces the start of a new hunting season; forty seasons later, no matter how my approach to hunting differs from when I was younger, venery lives inside of me like a strong woman calling.

A recital of fall-colored feathers concealing a soft-boiled, egg-shaped body weighing less than a thought, bob-whites are baffling. How does something that soft, seemingly without a muscle in its body, run and fly so fast? Terror, perhaps. From somewhere a description returns to me: "Quail leave the ground with the speed of a snipe, the sound of a partridge, and twist through the trees like demented wood-cock."

Bobwhites remind me of Hungarian partridge, birds that run up mountains faster than mule deer, rise in front of a pointing dog with the same clamor of wings, feel just as soft in the hand, and have, when they glide across the prairie, the same wing set. If I could hunt only two species of birds they would be the gray-legged partridge on a canvas of infinite perspectives and the bobwhite quail in my backyard.

The settings for my hunts have replaced the number of birds I kill, and because I hunt behind pointing dogs, covey birds offer more to see. I am becoming more of a bird-watcher than a bird-hunter. While I won't stop hunting, my priorities have shifted. Watching a belted kingfisher beat a brim to death on a tree limb interests me more than making a right and left double on quail. I suppose it is because I have not seen as many fish-beating birds as I have made doubles in my life.

This morning I thought I saw leaves falling from the pecan tree in the yard, but it was a dozen sparrows flying down from the tree's branches to where the nuts lay broken on the ground, and flying back up again, unlike any leaves I'd ever seen. My paleontologist friend thinks of birds as beautiful lizards. I tell him a birder is a voyeur and I qualify, having at one point or another keyholed the private quarters of some pretty and not-so-pretty women.

The exquisite pleasure I derive from watching birds through the lenses of my binoculars, full-sized birds stylized like those in the paintings of Gould and Selby, Thorburn and Audubon, is more fun than writing, so I write very little and watch a lot. I don't keep a count because I am more interested in what birds do. But just because I'm amused when I see a grackle shitting on a cardinal loitering around the feeders and am charmed at a dove's offering its mate a kernel of corn, does that mean I will feel differently about shooting this fall? The answer is no, not in the slightest. I will kill doves and quail and a turkey or two just as quickly as I wring the necks of the chickens and guineas I raise and with the same dispatch I use to ship a dozen pigs each year to the slaughterhouse. While these animals are under my care I feed them corn and overripe melons and bread and the remains of what I eat. When I feed them I watch them play and fight and try to mate and it makes me happy, but when the time is right I kill them and eat them and that makes me just as happy.

I can't shoot deer for having crippled a couple when

I was growing up, but Bill Poppell loves to hunt them, and most of the deer he or his friends shoot feeds members of the community who need the meat; the rest goes to others who don't need the meat but love to eat it. I won't deny that I derive a certain pleasure from the act of killing the birds I spend all year raising, but who is to say that I don't love my animals as much as the next man, or that my pleasure is more ill founded than the pleasure of eating a double burger is to another? Are there people out there so spiritually in tune with the animal world that they categorically know it isn't better for my pigs and deer and birds to have lived and died than not to have lived at all? I think not.

The humane societies have taken advantage of our gun-flexing attitude and made great strides in implementing their agendas. They want nature to be restored, but fight against one of nature's fundamental rules. In nature, the cruelty displayed by the hunter is a passing moment, an accepted entity, the reason why animals do not grow old in the wild. Yet the animal-rights people plod on, entrenched in their own vision of a world that never existed, a world they have conjured up with the same religious fanaticism of the deer whackers. Nature suffers while these extremes in stupidity argue and howl at each other with the fervor and rage of the mentally imbalanced.

The bobwhite's softness and shape encourage the viewer to imagine its fears, including visions of fangs and talons tearing into flesh. Coveted by snakes and skunks before they are even born, bobwhites gather strength from a collective fear that in the presence of danger immobilizes them as a whole and then triggers a loud and chaotic escape, meant to startle and confuse whatever threatens them.

The birds that have survived this far have a 60 percent chance of surviving until spring. The weak and the foolhardy are dead, and the survivors live in communal bliss. A cold November storm blew reams of golden leaves to the forest floor. Perhaps the old birds in the coveys remember this change of scenery as a transition time between the soft mast rotting on the ground and the hard mast as yet unfallen from the trees, a continuance of the vegetal year and a preview of winter, when that same hard mast sifts and hides on the forest floor and the legumes are cold and underground. Maybe the old birds also remember this as a season of added terrors, the terrors of dog and man.

I pumped gas next to a farmer who was going through hard times. His eyes looked beyond me. He was so far away in heart that he didn't know what day of the week it was, but he wanted to know about the birds. I said, "The drought is fixing to kill the young ones."

He nodded and said, "Good day," and drove away.

There is no reason to explain to a farmer why there are good quail years and poor quail years. He knows. He understands that no matter how well one manages the land, God is weather. In recent years the Bible Belt farmers and their families prayed for rain and lenient bankers, with an equal lack of success. As a newcomer to the game I curse and shake my fists above my head; so far that hasn't worked either.

IV

No one can have the part of me I give to my dogs. A gift as safe as loving a child, or for some as loving Christ; a part of me I guard carefully because it bears on my sanity. My dogs forgive the asshole in me, the anger in me, the arrogance in me, the brute in me. They forgive everything I do before I forgive myself. For me, the life and death of a dog is a calendar of time passing. I dream about my dogs, but recently the dreams have been turning into nightmares. One recurring scenario finds me hunting with Robin, the spaniel, on the ridge of a steep talus slope overlooking the Snake River in Idaho. The bitch runs after a cripple and follows the bird over the edge of the cliff. In my dream I watch Robin fall away, seemingly forever, a small tumbling figure against a mosaic of sagebrush, wheat, alfalfa fields, and water thousands of feet below. More recently I dreamed that suddenly, and with no warning, the same dog began shrinking, shrinking and barking and running in tiny circles around my feet, growing smaller and smaller, her eyes huge and brown and imploring. I threw my hat over her mouse-sized body but missed, and when she was the size of a fly she flew away.

I don't know what these dreams mean, but if they are meant to prepare me for my dog's eventual death I would like to remind my psyche that the bitch is only five years old, and to lay off for a while. On the other hand, perhaps these dreams are preparing me for my own death, or are fed by the guilt I feel when I kill something as beautiful and enviable as a bird. In any case, I'm sure that the communion I have with dogs should be channeled to my peers. However, as I think of man as the creator of desolation and not the center of reality, I don't, and I accept as a by-product of that choice the longing of loneliness, and the dark dreams that follow.

December 1, 1989

I wait in the front seat of my car next to a four-month-old puppy for ducks to fly out of a flooded hardwood pond on the edge of Lake Jackson. A cold fall morning without a gun. This time I hunt with a different perspective on life after spending time in southern Florida. I do this by sitting and watching wild things pass by. The sun, which broke quickly into the pale gray sky, hangs a few inches above the lake, shedding clouds until the water turns red. When the clouds burn off, the white sun resumes its ascent into the sky. The desperation I feel every time I venture into cities passes, even though not a duck creases the sky. The young dog, Robin, sits next to me with her head out the window, her ears opened to the fecund sounds of the marsh.

Back at the lake by 5 P.M. The puppy sits on my lap and stares out the front window, trembling. When the darkness gains weight the wood ducks fly back from the open water of the lake to roost and Robin follows their outline until the upholstery blocks her view. The ducks are reduced to long-winged shadows falling from the sky. In the backwater under the hardwoods, the ducks squeal and stir the mud, exciting the puppy. Wood ducks are my favorite table duck, and my least favorite to shoot because they are beautiful and dumb: male-model ducks.

Lake Jackson has turned purple again, purple water supporting a red horizon. Robin stares through the windshield at mosquitoes big enough to be birds. I am at my best when the sounds of civilization are at their lowest decibel and envy the fellow who, along with his Nagra tape recorder, hunted and found all the places in the world where the sounds were purely natural and nonhuman. He only found a handful, but there he made beautiful music.

A cold wind pushes night into the car. Robin shivers and curls up on my lap. On the way home the headlights play under the pine trees. Rock and roll fills the cab. I feel young again for having been alone with the dog, the birds, and now the music. Just before I fall asleep the puppy lays her head on my chest to let me know our day together is over, and then she moves as far from my restless sleeping habits as she can and still share the same bed.

My second dog is a seven-year-old lemon-and-white English pointer I bought four years ago as a broke bird dog. Mabel lived in a kennel before I bought her and now sleeps in a chair in my bedroom. I have spent four years hunting for Mabel instead of hunting for birds; four years of howling at her to come and watching her run 180 degrees away from me into the quagmires of neighboring counties. The dog doesn't mean to run away, but the moment the terrain is in any way at odds with her ability to see me, she becomes confused and then lost, incapable of figuring out from which direction I am calling. This happens because Mémé is dumb, dumb as a knot, dumber than the dumbest human being I have ever known, and a graduate of Spark College, the modern, electrically oriented school of dog training.

I should have sent her back to her previous owner, or at least given her to a retired social worker. The dog loves children and women; they in turn enjoy dressing her up in their clothes. Instead I persevered under the assumption that because she loved me she would one day recognize the sound of my voice as a rallying point and not the echo of dementia. She never has, and now that she is middle-aged she has taken to pissing in the puddle of water she drinks from, licking the fertilizer in the flower beds, and eating toads. I, of course, have taken to feeling sorry for her.

It has been said that a pointer that comes when called is rarer than an honest judge, to which one should add that compliance is not the compelling reason for owning a bird dog in the first place. Bred and trained to hunt with their senses screwed to the bone, they are designed to raise the level of quail hunting to an art form, and when things are right, they do. A breeze ruffling a handful of feathers carries enough weight to enslave a dog to a bird in a covenant of uneasy immobility. Setters, Britannys, and German shorthairs face quail as if their lives depended on it, but when a good English pointer faces a bird he does so with all but one foot on the coals of hell.

To counteract two demanding and jealous bitches, I have recently brought into the house an eight-week-old equalizer: a roan-colored dog with white whiskers, a black nose, black eyes, and best of all, a pair of nuts. His name is Carnac, the first male dog I have owned since I was sixteen years old. Carnac is a French Brittany that looks like a suckling pig, a roan-colored suckling pig that keeps its eyes on mine or on my hands, the hands that feed him and smack his ass. I turn him belly up sometimes, and point his tiny dick at the bitches to prepare them for his leadership a year from now. The little man-dog already likes to bite them in the ass and then run like hell, barking with joy. Once in a while the bitches catch him, pin him down, and make him pay, but because he is a male they mostly put up with his puppyhood. Carnac is a happy dog, willing and able to piss on any carpet and hump a woman's leg, displaying via the abandon of his grasp the keenness of his will. Now, if only he will hunt . . .

V

I remember reading about the old days, when Southern quail were abundant and time was cheap and hunting was an honorable diversion, when bird dogs spent most of the year as glorious bags of teats and bones, pups raised under slat-board porches and tended to until the sounds of acorns crackling under tractor tires snapped them to their feet, fired up their genes, and drove them to the woods. Dogs were bird dogs, English pointers, whose real reason for being was to stop the instant the scent of a quail intercepted their olfactory paths. What actually happened in terms of training between the time the bitch rose from her eight-month slumber to the time she splendidly addressed covey after covey of bobwhite quail, forgetting herself to everything except the birds and the men she was hunting for, was not specified, leaving me with a picture of cynegetic aplomb and grace.

Once in a great while, albeit not for very long, I have a desire to own an all-age, field-trial dog, a crackerjack flamenco dancer with quick feet, a flaring nose, and a whalebone rib cage; a dog that owns the ground it runs on and the wind on which birds fly. I want a dog whose casts give reason to the landscape, a dog that shakes at the delirium of discovery and imposes on birds the fortitude of its resolve; I covet the bag of bones that each fall metamorphoses into a greyhound. I covet the magician, the trickster, but I also want it to come when I call, and that is asking much too much. All-age dogs are the savants of the field-trial world, and asking them to do something as mundane as coming on command is like asking van Gogh to add a cow to the landscape.

For a moment in time, twenty years ago, I hunted bobwhite quail from horseback behind those kinds of dogs. Memories return in the shape of thin, black men riding fast Southern horses, men who worked the flanks and signaled points by raising their caps above their heads, and uncanny dog handlers who smelled birds before the dogs. I remember galloping to points with my heart in my throat for fear of not getting to the covey before it blew up. I hunted behind all-age dogs that had competed in, and in some cases won, national championships; dogs that trembled at the mere mention of birds, dogs that presented to the guns a quarry whose head they were given to eat. Memories of those days also include races between horsemen and deer across broomsedge fields, of old dogs found pointing swamp birds under the radiance of a cold winter moon, of gentlemen who only killed male quail, and of dark-skinned women whose favors were as warm as the biscuits they baked.

A quote taken from the guest book at Sehoy Plantation, Alabama, December 13, 1967:

> Flushed twenty-seven coveys of quail, shot over twenty-three. Filled two limits. My companion missed all but one bird. Pointers, stretched to a beautiful attitude. Kennel mates backing in perfect unanimity of opinion. Tipped a bobwhite or two out of each covey rise. Moses [name of black dog handler] exclaimed, "Gents, that covey's powerful close." Ate fried quail, collard greens with pepper vinegar, lima beans, hot rolls and French wine. Port with dessert, Cognac later. Bid six hearts, finessed the jack, and made the slam. A day to remember.

Dogs, like men, lose their range and enthusiasm for life from having the wildness in them questioned. In the case of dogs, trainers these days ask the questions with single-digit probes of electric trauma, trauma that reaches its destination faster than the trainer's thought. When sustained, and with the range to reach across fields and dales, this bolt of bionic inhumanity will scramble a dog's brains and walk the sonofabitch to hell and back. In the hands of most men the electronic collar serves a number of purposes ranging from expressing suppressed hate to being a genuine training tool. The obvious shortcut electricity provides is not unlike sound bites and fast foods, and allows questionable trainers to post-pone working a client's dog almost indefinitely. In the hands of a good man the collar removes the boot and the leather strap from the routine of training, and when applied just right can make the dog believe that God is watching and its salvation rests with its trainer. A thin line. One application too many and the client owns a round-eyed dog that pisses in the water it drinks.

I am a terrible dog trainer because the trait I like in dogs is the same I like in men: namely, civil disobedience. Training is repetition; hell is toeing the line. I have witnessed extreme punishment applied to dogs with instruments ranging from a thirty-second hold on a number-five button to a two-by-four. When I was much younger and fresh out of Europe, where field trials were and still are thought of as civilized sporting contests between reasonable men and women and their dogs, I sucker-punched a dog trainer at a field trial in Pennsylvania for jerking a full-grown Labrador off its feet by its ears. The dog had swum the wrong course at a dead duck. I drilled the asshole in the ear and he pitched face first in the mud. My British host, without so much as raising an eyebrow, patted the dog on the head, looked down at the man, and said, "Well, as he's in no position to answer you, we might as well be moving along. Cruel bugger, what?"

The breeding program for bird dogs in this country has historically been geared to the field-trial competitions, and specifically to those dogs in the high-octane category, dogs with speed and endurance, dogs that cast to the far reaches of sanity and flow across the landscape like music, orchestrating their quest with a batonlike tail, and do so with more style and purpose than their brace mates.

The sometimes heedless and always presumptuous experiment that breeders wallow into in order to fashion winners is line breeding. When successful, line breeding produces dogs whose bird-finding acrobatics are those of perfectly controlled madness. When unsuccessful, which is most of the time, some or all of the tainted traits in the bloodlines surface, as was the case in the thin-lipped, tight-assed noble blood of Europe before the revolution. Extreme line breeding, standard in most kennels, goes hand in hand with extreme culling.

The experiments in genetics performed by the monk Gregor Mendel in his kitchen garden over a hundred years ago are mathematically so simple to understand that anyone, including my neighbor, is convinced that he can build a better dog, a super-dog, one that will win the Ames Plantation field trials and make him famous. To that purpose, mother and son, father and daughter, sister and brother are Osterized into a gene-pool stew by stubborn men and women with egos the size of beer kegs and brains the size of seeds. Once in a while, a man with a vision and a man blessed with the perfect touch comes along—in this century that man is Bob Wehle; his dogs are English pointers and his bloodlines originate with a dog named Elhew—and God-dogs claw their way out of otherwise malformed litters. But as a rule, line breeding does not include a scientific horoscope that can predict whether the dog will be a monster or the reincarnation of Rin Tin Tin. The bottom line is, when dogs are born with two dicks and teeth growing through their nose, it is time to heed the wisdom of one's mother, genetic decency, or even the corrupt but lucrative practices of thoroughbred racing, and listen to the plaintive howls of civilizations whose leaders had similar designs.

Some years ago, a good-looking French dog-trainer and I watched a bitch Labrador I had driven three hundred kilometers to buy being serviced by a littermate, by error, because the hospitable breeder had invited me into her converted farmhouse for a glass of wine, some cheese, olives, a plate of crudités, Normandy butter, and a loaf of bread. While we ate and the siblings got acquainted, the dark-haired trainer with freckles on her nose got my attention by biting into a pickle and stating, "If cooking is the foreplay, swallowing is the orgasm." Now, half an hour later, confronted with incest and the sure loss of a sale, she held the palms of her hands to the sky and said, "In this business there is too much line breeding and not enough imagination." Taking that as a cue of sorts, I scooped her up in my arms—she was tiny—and, along with my imagination, trotted up the stairs to her bedroom.

VI

The best dog is one that adapts to its master's temperament and style of hunting, and while I marvel at the English pointers and setters, such dogs have always tiptoed beyond the horizons of my hearing within hours of my owning them, and from that moment on I have had to blow up my face to get their attention. Now that I have retired my sneakers they are no longer right for me. I want a dog that hunts about a hundred yards or so on either side of me and passes within gun range each time it checks in. I usually have an idea where the birds are and would just as soon have Biff go where I tell him to. Not a workable agenda when dealing with the tightly strung violins of dogdom.

Now, when I hunt, I like to think about things like

how the trees have grown, the last time I slept with a strange woman, the direction of the wind, and what wine I'm going to drink with dinner; killing is a formality. When I hunt with another person, I want to listen to and talk to that person— otherwise I wouldn't hunt with him. I want to stop if I choose to without losing the dog or having to hack at it to keep it on a level course. I have done all those things, and after a decade of getting just as pissed off as I did when I played golf, I bought the Brittany with hopes that I won't feel the fingers of retribution crawl up my backside each time the dog is out of sight. It all comes down to the man and what he wants from his dog. In my case I plan to hunt behind pointers and setters until the day I retire my guns, but they will belong to someone else.

One can argue that, performed with a measure of dignity and restraint, hunting is just as important an issue now as it was three hundred years ago, but for opposite reasons. Hunting is no longer a survival issue for man, but has become a survival issue for the game, because while we have multiplied like rabbits, the game has dwindled tenfold. Our importance as hunters lies in the fact that we as individuals, without affiliations to anything or anyone other than the sport, witness and assess the condition of the game and habitat in this country. Our credentials are that we are out there, in nature, when others are not, and that we are out there because we want to be, not because we have to or are paid to be. Our eyes solicit the traceries of spoors on the earth and of birds in the sky; our spirits are conscious of ravens and long for the restitution of wolves and bears to the land. We are the wildlife thermometers, poking about in rivers and swamps, in the shadows of forest canopies, under the flashes of desert suns, and the force that drives us is our soul.

We hunters, more than any other group on earth, should understand the symbiotic relationship between species and how it has come to pass that, thanks to our destructive meddling, the reflection of a teal on a pond is no longer free of charge. Those of us who understand the complex nature of a teal's life, the protection and food needed to grow the feathers that send that image darting over the water, also understand what the chase and the kill do to the spirit of man, their rewards and their shames. Because we understand and feel these things more acutely than our peers, it is sacrilegious of us not to protect with all our might what resources remain to be saved. If we neglect our obligations, we deserve the contempt of generations to come.

VII

I have done some shameful things in the name of sport in the past forty years, and I recognize in my not-so-distant past the genetic chimpanzee in me. When Robin wasn't quite a year old I picked her up by the scruff of the neck and with just enough anger in me to sicken the act, threw her to the ground. The dog had been running around in a dove field enjoying her youth, the sounds of gunfire, and the sight of falling birds while I, infuriated at her disobedience, wanted her to sit by my side. Robin fell wrong and screamed like a baby. She wasn't as hurt as she was terrified by the fact that the one being in the world she loved unconditionally had suddenly and for no apparent reason turned on her. It scared me for all the appropriate reasons, not the least of which was that

I recognized in me the dog trainer I had knocked to the ground years before. Nowadays when the little bitch lays her head on my shoulder in the dark of night it is because I have called her to me, waking from the nightmare of that act; waking from the dream in which I had broken her neck.

The same crass and impulsive behavior incited me to shoot sparrows and swallows as a child, crows and hawks when I should have known better, and more recently a bobcat in the back and a raccoon in the face. My unbecoming and violent nature as a child doesn't concern me anymore. I have forgiven myself for being a young man with a young man's rules. But now that I am, for better and for worse, tired—no, exhausted—from witnessing the insipid venality that conjures up violence in men, these questions of ethics so easily dismissed a few years ago weigh me down for reasons of principle, age, and change. What I forgave in the past I don't anymore, and it is not that I am uncomfortable in my role of predator. I fully understand the nature of hunting and being hunted, eating, sleeping, and procreating. In fact my inclination toward reclusiveness nudges me further and further into the world of animals, and I have to constantly guard against letting myself regress into a medium that functions with even less thought than the one I see in the streets and watch on television. My dog's voice belongs to a dog and I am not meant to take it personally. On the other hand, I know deep in my heart that there is something basically wrong about killing for pleasure.

The day I shot a bobcat instead of a turkey I altered the natural progression of life by killing for no reason. The cat walked out of the woods, I raised the gun and pulled the trigger. The act was a simple one. A response to the knowledge of the cat's predilection for turkey, but one I deeply regretted when I ran my hand over the tawny-colored coat of the adult female, tough and sinewy from making a living and dropping litters but now lifeless and flat on a bed of dirt in the shade of a sweet-gum tree with a .22-caliber Hornet hole in her heart. There was a time when killing the bobcat would have pleased me. I would have felt like the protector, the benevolent despot of the forest. Now I question what it means to meddle in things that are so much more natural than what I see on the news. I feel like a half-wit to have in me the same senseless traits I reproach in others, particularly as I am no longer convinced that I am better than the cat. Killing for no reason is killing with malice.

A month later, driving down a dirt road overlooking a pasture, I stopped and, from inside the car, shot a raccoon in the face while it watched me from inside the fork of a dogwood tree. The raccoon fell slowly, raking the bark with its claws, holding on to life until gravity took hold and pulled it to where it would eventually rot. I had just finished reading an article about how raccoons rob quail nests.

The seduction of the scope made for simple killing and emotional ambiguity. Physical magnification stole the life from the image and left me with a sharp target. The precision of glass is finite, but the consequence of a senseless death is not, except in how it takes its toll on the psyche of man. Could it be that those unnatural killings—I didn't eat or use either animal—were attempts at killing the wildness in myself?

VIII

December 15, 1992

The full moon is framed by the top of the loblolly pines that flank the pond house. The moon robs the stars of their light. I listen to the night and once again pray for rain; weather makes grown men throughout the South hunker down with rock-hard plugs of chew in the sides of their mouths. At the gas station, young men tug at their nuts through the crotch of their pants and forecast the weather in loud voices. They talk on and on, so that when something does happen one of them can say, "I told you so!" The older men spit and shut up. They know all there is not to know about weather.

The water in the pond is not up to the dock yet and

the bottom is full of tall brown weeds that look a little like picked cotton. A quarter of a mile to the northeast the structure of the new dam rests like a tremendous black log in the water, large enough to hold back the floods of Judea, or so it seems. Words such as *permits, specifications, decrees, fines,* and *board meetings* entered and left my life, as did the United States government, but my name and the name of my farm is in its repository, sandwiched among other files like felonious fingerprints, for the rest of time.

Yesterday I asked Bill to butcher two piglets from the sounder of eleven the sow dropped two months ago. "There won't hardly be enough meat to eat," he says.

"Ever hear of suckling pigs?"

Bill nodded.

"I need to have them weigh between twelve and fifteen pounds, dressed."

He shook his head. The waste of meat was an indulgence. "In that case," he said, "we'll butcher them here. Won't cost a thing. Little porkers like that; hell, we'll kill 'em, scald 'em, rub the hair off their hides, and make them ready in an hour. Won't be nothing to eat, though."

The next day Bill adjusted a hammer to the heads of two twenty-pounders. The piglets never made a sound. Their siblings went on about the business of eating corncobs without paying the slightest attention to the quivering bodies, didn't even smell them. The water in the boiler was kept just under boiling and after the pigs were run through it their bristles rubbed off with a brush of the hand. Under the coarse hair the skin was just as white and smooth as a baby's. Bill removed the hard coating on the hooves, a plug of wax out of each ear, checked the livers—but they were wormy—and tried to talk me into eating the oysters. I passed. Bled and gutted the pigs weighed twelve pounds. Castrated and a year later they would have weighed three hundred.

There is a great deal to be said about patience, but there is also something to be said about slow-cooked suckling pig rubbed with fruit preserves, hot peppers, soy, and garlic.

IX

In December the white-tailed bucks run does until their hinds are dark with sweat and they stand shaking and exhausted, surrendering to the insistence of the reproductive process. It is the beginning of deer-hunting season in Gadsden County, and just like everywhere else, the deer take a beating without much thought given to the well-being of the herd.

My neighbor's motto (as it is with all the Bubbas in the Union) is a truculent "Shoot the shit out of dem sumsabitches." A sorry state of obtuse thinking for a species about to celebrate the two-thousandth anniversary of the birth of a spiritual leader who advocated compassion.

Shooting deer in Florida is almost always practiced from a tree house, or stand, overlooking a mound of corn, beets, sweet potatoes, or anything else deer enjoy eating. Not to be confused with hunting, which by definition is the pursuit of game, this passive involvement with nature includes waiting, watching, and shooting; it is not hunting in the same manner that shooting doves is not hunting. Seeking, searching, chasing, ferreting out, or even casting aimlessly about the woods as I do applies to hunting. Sitting on one's ass waiting for an animal to come to bait is just that: sitting on one's ass, wearing dirty-looking outfits. The skills most sought after in this endeavor are immobility and the ability to shoot a bullet inside the radius of a Ping-Pong paddle at a hundred yards.

However, the ambushing of game (and man) coming to food and to water holes is as old as predation. And although elitists like me look down upon the sport as a form of mendacity, it has its merits, particularly for the voyeurs, the listeners, and the dreamers. Whenever I really want to get personal with nature I'll sit in a tree stand and wait. I'll wait as long as it takes for the entire natural world within the radius of my sight to manifest itself, and if I wait long enough and sit quietly enough I'll fool nature's tenants into resuming their lives unaware of the peeper in the tree, the peeper who by virtue of being alone with his beginnings feels a deep joy and pride in being alive and in a position to observe what others couldn't care less about.

A few days before the deer season, my neighbor, Sergeant B. J. Pruit, calls on some friends and in a party atmosphere sight-in their rifles, crank some rounds, and suck on belly beers. The party starts slowly, a shot every five minutes or so, a walk to the target, a debate on velocity, elevation, grain, and powder—all the specifics that excite hunters. But as the afternoon lengthens and the beers settle and the time between drinking and pissing shortens, the tension on the range quickens and the momentum builds to a crescendo. Volleys of bullets scream through the air, bury into trees, fracture empty cans, fly aimlessly into clouds; shoulders ache, eyes redden, foam builds, and rational thought evaporates. Just before dark the countryside is at war with itself and afterward, long after the sun has dropped behind the last tree stump, a final salvo is loosened by those who simply can't stop pulling on the trigger; undoubtedly the same nucleus of men virulently terrified that the prerogative of shooting at the night may one day be taken away.

In Texas I witnessed a fine example of sporting impatience at a camp where the deer feeders—erected on metal derricks, exactly one hundred yards from the tree stands—are automatic and noisy. Twice a day a pound or two of corn is loosened out of a solar-activated grain-spreader onto a plot of bare, sandy earth, a stage of coagulated blood hardened by the hooves of a thousand deer. Before the sound of the cogwheels has faded in Norman Nimrod's ears, deer and turkey race out of the mesquite mottes to get a first lick at a purposefully scant amount of flying food. The shooter waits for the grinding of the gears to end and lets fly one hundred and eighty grains of lead at the biggest deer, forks over two thousand dollars to the smiling owner, and heads for home, full of temporary cheer and a flushing kinship with Daniel Boone. However, as there is no way of posing for a picture with a dead animal without looking retarded, the feeling eventually passes and the picture yellows on the wall. Death soils the best intentions and that is why blood and agony work best on the six o'clock news.

X

December 11, 1993

The acorns, which fell early this year, predicted a cold winter, as did the hornet nests, built very close to the ground. Misty treetops hidden in the fog. Meadowlarks work the fields, confusing the dogs. On overcast days the sky falls all the way to earth. Autumn's bearing is one of lingering death.

Two weeks ago a storm blew across the pond and stripped a sweet-gum tree of a year's worth of living by hurling its leaves into the water. Golden reflections raced over the choppy gray surface and disappeared like shoals of shiners into the bulrushes.

High-flying cirrus clouds curl over the state with regularity, and the insects that are not otherwise transfixed by the cold hibernate under a scale of time. Freezes deepen the silences of night. Early in the morning when dew beads the spiderwebs and fog washes the shadows away, the kudzu vines hang lifeless from the trees like the rigging of becalmed sailing ships. The quail, even the squealers, are full-grown and have chosen their retinue. I run the dogs for a week without carrying a gun. We work the heart out of the mornings and, hiding behind trees, under leaves, and high in the sky, the eyes of nature track our progress. The sky never reneges on its deadly promises to quail.

The discoloration of fall and the comportment of the dogs, casting with rural determination ahead of me, reestablishes the conviction that simplicity wears well. I celebrate that simplicity every time I hunt.

The dogs investigate beneath the wax myrtle bushes, the briars, the boundaries of fallow fields, and the edges of wet-weather ponds, where they startle an occasional snipe. They mouse in the grass like puppies because this is the first week of the season and I'm not carrying a gun. Sorting out game-bird smells from the distractions of an undergrowth as yet untamed by frost is not easy and at best requires a limbering of the muscles, a sharpening of the senses, and the remembrances of years past.

The coveys we flush stretch their wings on a free ride to safety, profiting for having survived the encounter. Compared to walking down a city street, the vegetable hindrances, the vines, and the amateurish dog work is good stuff. In my strange and unyielding domain I fall, as I do every autumn, for nature's seductive solicitations.

A family of coyotes howls at the moon. My wife runs outside and gathers her baby white cat in her arms, scared for its life. Two years ago, a similar commotion turned out to be a wild bobcat pacing the length of the swimming pool into which it had convinced my wife's old cat to swim or be eaten. The bobcat ran into the night while I dragged the old cat out by its tail, sleek and hissing. That afternoon I took it to the vet's, where it was put to sleep; the cancer growing in its colon, I was told, had spread and nothing more could be done without adding insult to its pain. I buried the cat next to the pond but, reflecting on the irony of the bobcat's timing, I dug the grave too shallow. A week later a hole in the earth was all that was left of the cardboard box that had served as a coffin. I convinced myself that the wildcat had found the burial site and enjoyed its meal after all.

A rain shower later, I found a perfect spearhead inches from the empty grave. The white flint stone was two and a half inches long, two inches wide, and shaped like a sagittate oak leaf. The hunter who had carved it four hundred or so years before had used a deer antler to shave and shape each facet before lashing it to a hickory shaft. The tip on this specimen was intact, which led me to guess that the spear either found the soft tissues of a mammal that got away or rode the wind and landed on a blanket of grass. In either case the flint stone remained hidden, and, like a seed, lay dormant for centuries waiting to be disturbed by the rain and me. I have found dozens of Indian artifacts since I moved to the farm, mostly from the Lower Creek tribes that lived in the area, but also from Appalachees and the nomadic Cherokees. There are half a dozen springs on the farm, and that's where I go looking for the past after it rains. Finding an unbroken arrowhead is akin to finding a perfect seashell after a storm; to muse about the man or woman who carved it adds weight to its beauty.

XI

No matter how much I enjoy raising, feeding, and tending to birds during the year, the time comes each fall when the urge to shoot them drives me out the door, gun in hand, shells in pockets, and dogs running amok. It will take a couple of weeks before I shoot with any degree of certainty, but that doesn't deter me from heading into the woods with a minimum of mercy in my soul. Whatever notions of farming linger have shifted to the harvest mode. Hunt them, shoot them, and cook them are the entries on my agenda.

A gun in hand alters the nature of any walk. Hunting requires a target; walking doesn't. I have spent most of my life hunting empty thickets, convinced the next one would contain a windfall of birds. Forty years later I still follow the trim footprints of quail into the brushy Braille of their hiding places, but now, for reasons of age and time, I differentiate between a quest and a promenade. If I am carrying a weapon it is because I want to use it; otherwise I'd rather carry my binoculars and watch birds behave like lizards.

As far as my dogs are concerned the wavering predator in me has finally approved of their time in the field. Dogs, like young men, need as much field time as they can steal. I remember with nostalgia and a certain envy the years I wouldn't sleep the night before the opening of the hunting season. They were good years, driven years, when the only reason I gave a damn if the sun rose or not was for it to shed enough light on a stretch of river or marsh or corner of woods to shoot or fish by. A sacred fire burned like a beacon up my ass and I cannot begin to explain how much I miss those fires and all the other fires that pushed the young man in me in search of adventure.

I have shot wood pigeons out of tree houses, red grouse over lavender moors, and thrush in cherry orchards; I have lost black ducks to sharks, snipe to alligators, and quail to snakes, and in each case I reveled in the moment just as I reveled in the far more numerous moments of my sporting life when I never saw a thing. In one respect I am lucky to have lived during an era when game was thought of by all but the scientific community and a handful of blue-haired old ladies as plentiful, if not unlimited, and if it has taken me all these years to inquire further into the matter it is because it took that long for my callous eyes to soften and my manly heart to bleed.

I now wish fewer birds had flown over the barrels of my guns, but twenty years ago I sincerely wished for more. Birds were targets, and in those days targets were the tangibles that differentiated one man from the next—vanity shooting prevails for many to this day—and, being a streak shooter, I took my good days for granted and raged at my bad ones. In the betting man's world of target shooting my temper always got the better of me, but from one day to the next I was a good predator and killed my share of game.

Shooting well is the result of a repetitive process, beginning with a long apprenticeship and culminating in the ability to kill well. Crippling is anathema to all who care about the sport, not to mention the irrefutable argument of those who are against it. I still take stupid, vain shots inspired only by the passing fancy of my ego. The bird that takes shot and lives through the dog work is not going to die a pleasant death. I usually shoot a 28-gauge, but there is a lot to be said about a light, open-bore 12-gauge that throws a broad pattern and a lot of shot out of a short shell. The point is to lay down what one aims at, to get the killing over with as expediently as possible and move on.

My shooting motivation has come full circle, from relishing the hard shot to looking for the easy one, the one that doesn't cripple. When I hunt quail by myself I defer to my dog's point and watch the covey disperse through the trees without raising the gun. I shoot at what we refer to as down here as the sleepers, the laggards that get up after the fact. First and foremost I want to see a mess of quail get up in front of the dogs, but I kill sleepers because they are the weakest birds in the gene pool and the easiest to hit. There is a chance that by picking such birds I am culling genetically in-ferior quail—certainly the slowest specimens in the covey—but the truth is that this game allows me to stretch my pleasure while doing the least amount of harm to the population.

When friends visit and we are three, I stand twenty yards behind the point. Again, I get to watch the dogs, the rising covey, and the shooting. More often than not a quail breaks back and offers an interesting shot. The first year I was here I only shot at cock birds, a frustrating exercise. I don't see as well as I used to and cannot pick a white mask out of a covey well enough to be consistent. Also, the concentration required to find the right bird dampened the rhythm in my normally instinctive shooting. So the pot remained empty.

When two of us are hunting the procedure is stan-dard, except in rough cover, when I'll often send the spaniel in to flush. The pointing dogs don't seem to mind and it allows us to position ourselves for the best shots. Neither my friends nor I kill very many birds; we walk too slowly and talk too much. My shooting ability has waned along with my con-centration, which has decreased proportionately with my de-sire to kill. Pulling the trigger is now the least important word on the page and the best excuse I can think of for shooting poorly.

XII

I believe that, discounting those who hunt for survival—
and there are many in this country who still do—and
those who are new at the game and hunt on young legs
and jacked-up glands, the rest of us, and certainly those of us
who have shot and shot and shot again over long lifetimes,
should consider spending more time hunting with binoculars
or a camera or, better yet, with the grace of a teacher. When
killing is no longer imperative to the success of the endeavor,
the natural progression is from hunter to teacher, from player
to coach; the hunter becomes mentor, storyteller, a shaman to
the following generation. The hunting I have known was
better than my children's will be but not as good as my father's, and that holds true for most quests. The conditions

under which we hunted and the conditions under which we are going to hunt in the future must be explained to the young if we are to pass on any legacy at all. The original goal of the hunter was to gather food to survive. One could argue that the goal of the modern hunter is simply to enter the arena, an arena dwindling in size and population, but an arena that holds all the beauty and mystery of our heritage.

At a time when the wings of migration are beating against the black clouds of man's follies, at a time when 80 percent of our rivers are too polluted to swim in, at a time when garbage bags suffocate our reefs, wise men and women are needed to teach those who no longer care or understand how exquisite it once was.

The only true aristocracy is the
aristocracy of consciousness.
—D. H. Lawrence

Winter

Two inches of hard rain, followed by three mornings of
heavy frost, drove the remnants of fall underground.
The color green vanished from the landscape except
where wheat and clover pushed out of the brown earth in
rectangles and rivers of summer intensity. The saturated
ground had rotted all but the hardest seeds, stretching the
feeding range of the bobwhite quail. Pinecones fell when the
wind blew and the damp Spanish moss waved like molted
snakeskins from the bare branches of pecan trees.

The deformity of trees, their growths and fungus-re-
lated bulges, their scars, burns, and deer rubbings, stand
starkly against the gray skyline. At times, confused by a breath
of warm gulf air, a riot of yellow butterflies emerges from its

cocoon and dances above the benumbed weeds only to die at sunset. The bands of summer crickets have buried their vocal endowments for the winter, and except for a deadly complaint or two the nights are silent.

Profane as it may sound, one can create beauty with a chainsaw. The chaos of a Southern underbrush slowly growing into a hardwood forest has its visual merits, and more practically acts as a refuge for game seeking temporary peace. Accordingly, half a dozen areas on the farm never feel the heat of a spring fire, but from other areas I have removed thousands of trees, cutting those on the slopes—leaving the stumps to fight erosion—and pushing the rest over, roots and all, with gigantic steel machines.

I opened my woods in accordance with an immediate interest in diversification and a subjective twenty-year vision of its future. Young trees with potential are encouraged to grow old and good old trees are given room to expand by removal of the competition. To keep things visually interesting, I leave those trees that have struggled and won their contorted fight for sunlight. The manner in which this land is shaped allows me to see across one, two, sometimes three narrow valleys, on the shoulders of which we plant browntop millet, sorghum, or corn in rows and at angles one from another to take advantage of as many crooks and crannies as possible. These winter meanderings of food planted under a hot summer sun shed seeds until winter is almost done.

The plots are planted thick to provide cover as well as food. When Jim Buckner taught game management courses, he would tell his students to lie on their stomachs in front of, say, a patch of sorghum, and ask them to describe what they saw, which was exactly how a quail saw things. Kneeling, they saw through the eyes of a turkey; on their feet the students were apprentice managers again. But in the interim they had gained a certain depth of vision. Looking down on another species's lot is not conducive to empathy. Not surprisingly, just as with humans, survival usually comes down to the basics: groceries and shelter.

The work to produce wild quail is in itself artificial— just as artificial as everything else we do to "improve" nature, a presumptuous concept if ever there was one. In the case of bobwhites, I overfeed and overprotect a population that would otherwise balance itself within the natural habitat. On the other hand, the management gives my life a certain meaning, and creating habitat makes me feel good. In the long run, what I do with these birds will amount to nothing; interest will wane, the land will be sold, the earth will split open, and the floods will come. In the meantime, there is a similarity between my encouraging a population of quail to explode and the socially funded overpopulation of humans in cities. Quail, like urbanites, subsist on allocations.

For a month, late one winter, two large Caterpillars labored through my woods pushing over trees. The first one was a D-6 bulldozer preceded by a glistening, king-sized blade, a gladiator on steel tracks that traveled the softer bottoms devouring shade as it went. The second was a 762 loader guided by a bucket large enough to bury an elephant and propelled by four tremendous rubber tires, each one moving independently. The rubber-wheeled monster's job was to push the trees over and the crawler's to herd them into piles; the artistry of the operators was to skin as few good trees as possible in the process. The loader would raise its bucket, rest it on the trunk of its victim, and apply a force the tree had never envisioned. In the case of some black gums and iron-woods the loader would get up on its hindquarters shaking and snorting, occasionally falling back to earth where it would hunker down like a sumo wrestler, regain its breath, and try again. Some hardwoods won the war, returning from battle with scars on their trunks, but most times the tree would give, suddenly, and the monster would rip and snort and dance over its vanquished foe. All this was frightening, both in its physicality and because of the insolence it took to tamper with trees that in some instances were saplings when my children were born. On the other hand, where the machines passed, light followed, and scenes emerged like Dutch paintings appearing from behind the brown lacquer of time, in this case emerging from behind a tangle of fruitless trees.

The man who sat in the cab of the 762 loader was especially quick about moving around stumps and debris, choosing the trees he wanted, planning his shots like a pool player, visualizing the angles of fall and projecting three or four moves ahead. Both operators worked from seven-thirty in the morning to noon and from twelve-thirty to five-fifteen, stopping only for repairs. The man who worked the 762 was kind and cheerful and broad as a beer keg. He drove forty miles to and from work five days a week, and made less money than a city maid. At the end of the day when I'd ferry him back to his truck he would play with Robin and scratch her head with a huge finger, as gently as if she were a baby. "I just love dogs," he'd say fussing with her ears. "Come to think about it, I love all animals."

"How about trees, do you love trees?"

"Trees?" he repeated, smiling down at the dog licking his wrist. "You bet I do; they keep my kids in clothes."

Sculpting the land is not unlike sculpting the body, making it do something it wouldn't do under normal circumstances. But while the body can gorge itself back to obesity in a matter of weeks, thinning trees mandates a long hard look and some serious planning. Thanks to Bill and the operators I got lucky. The machines worked a total of sixty hours, awakened the forest to sunlight, and disturbed acres of legume seeds waiting for such an occasion to assert themselves. Creatures large and small took advantage of the windfall, and two years later (it takes two years for the earth to heal from such an operation) the understory is clean, the trees are strong, and it would be hard to find a scar.

In a few seasons the pine trees I have planted will take on an air of respectability. The fields will grow old and worn from my fires, the fluctuations of weather, and from hunting in them; the live oaks will assume even greater bearing from standing alone uncrowded. In the meantime, I will continue to push over the poor specimens and plant younger and straighter ones. There may or may not be an artistry to all this, but one thing is certain: the mistakes are memorable. The odds are that when everything looks right to me, I'll be dead, the rest of the world will be straddling the fence, and all the trees a man could want will sprout out of petri dishes for a lot less trouble.

II

I don't believe that the earth can support the weight of too many more souls, dreamless and blinded by the anguish of life, any more than it can support the poisons man invented for the betterment of his pocketbook. There are solutions, hundreds of solutions, but no way of implementing them because they have become, out of necessity, just as radical and painful as the practices that produced them. The farmer is not going to re-establish hedgerows until his bank loans are paid up, any more than the urban working class is going to stop eating guts and eyeballs ground into patties from cows that graze the burned-over rain forests of the Amazon, just because scientists jabber on about biodiversity, ozone craters, and rising seas.

A question then arises: How do we save our wildlife habitat when more and more parking lots are needed to house the cars that transport the parents to buy the food to feed the children who have never even dreamed of those beautiful places where birds sing?

One obvious answer, and one that concerns those of us who hunt, is the strength we can wield through our numbers, the symbiotic link between the natural world and the man on the street. Hunters are twenty million strong, twenty million voices, twenty million votes, twenty million bridges between business and politics, between material comfort and the decimation of our resources; a decimation that is no longer a moot point but a very real act of diminishing returns.

We hunters are the perfect conduits. Unfortunately our fraternity is just as split on conversation as the rest of the interested assemblies. It is going to take education, lots of education, because we are blessed with an incredible number of obtuse members whose balefully uneducated acumen and compassion is mirrored by my neighbor and his buddies.

The occipital muscle–flexing of the "Me Tarzan, you Jane" stream of consciousness that grinds out of B.J.'s and Bubba's mouths is enough to terrify the dullest dullard. To whack a deer, to drill a duck, to blast a bear are common gasconades—words that rhyme with nigger, kike, and spick—that when used repeatedly in the confines of a closed forum hail fascist loathing and mental imbalance. Hunting for many is an act of vengeance on a world that for millennia held the upper hand. For others it's a means of getting even with everyday life, one's boss, a difficult childhood, whimpering erections, or poor digestion, in ways and through acts that are paragons of brutality; behavior that since it is directed at animals goes unanswered. No one in the real world wants to deal with human baboons bearing guns, and in this day and age hunters shouldn't feign surprise or outrage when private landowners turn B.J. away along with his curs and his blast-and-cast approach to what used to be referred to as sport.

The birds we love to make fly in front of our dogs are disappearing, and regardless of what was accepted as gospel in the past, the argument that hunting does not impose duress on game no longer holds water. There is no disputing that the ravages of human expansion and pollution are the main culprits in the disappearance of wildlife and that the demise of an eleven-thousand-year tradition of man as hunter-gatherer can be partially blamed on the fact that we have run out of geography. But predation is also to blame, and not only in the form of talons and claws but in the form of lead, and more recently steel. Simply put, there are more guns, less game, insufficient food, and fewer places for the animals to hide. It stands to reason then that how we approach hunting in the immediate future carries both practical and moral implications.

I would suggest to those modern-day hunters, those patriots so outraged that their undeniable right to "bear arms" is in jeopardy, that they resign themselves to the fine art of compromise instead of braying that digits kill children and that guns don't. Because if they refuse to see what has happened to the social and natural structure of the world since the Constitution of this country was hammered out and insist on lamenting their diminished social standing in the eyes of the rest of society while continuing to make man-talk around the campfire, I believe that it will be only a matter of time before we live in a society so terrified that it will out of necessity amend the amendment, forbid the ownership of guns, and beg for a police state, period.

III

I have hunted with men who think of hunting as a contest between themselves and nature, others who kill to feed their families, and some who pit their abilities against whomever they are hunting with. I have hunted with safe hunters and dangerous hunters; some who cover as much ground as their feet will allow and others who are just as happy waiting for a partridge under the pear tree. The list is long and includes those who cared about the game and those who didn't. I prefer hunting with men who care, but count as friends many who, in every other walk of life are honorable and generous, but when it comes to hunting think nothing of pushing the autoloader out of the blind and killing five times their legal limit. It is as though everything in their lives is in harmony except for a troubled corner of their soul, a denied need, a suppressed anger for which the escape valve is the wanton destruction of what they most cherish and want to preserve.

I know and have hunted with an otherwise fine fellow who, in 1988, with the help of five scrambling boys, proved something vague to himself by shooting and retrieving a thousand Colombian doves in one day. So, what does that mean? Is it that these otherwise good and, in the cases I've mentioned, intelligent men have some closeted hatred? Were they abused as children? Or is it more primal, in the sense that when their blood is up they cannot stop until they run out of bullets or get caught. That any of the upper-class predators kills for the joy of killing is well documented and has caused, in many cases, an unmerciful pursuit by man. Perhaps some of us are closer to our evolutionary ancestry than we care to admit; perhaps the basic urge to kill, which we have attempted to curtail for the sake of civilized behavior, is awake and present. I don't know how it feels to kill a man, but I know what it takes to kill an animal and how I feel on those days when the birds fly just right and there are lots of them and I am shooting well and don't want to stop.

A few years ago I spent a day with two brothers who work as dog trainers on separate plantations in the vicinity of Tallahassee. Once or twice a year, toward the end of the hunting season, they are invited by different landowners to thin out the quail population and provide the owner with birds for the freezer. In defense of the landowner, the guests invited from faraway places to shoot during the regular hunting season are for the most part of a certain age and can't hit a damn thing; consequently, very few bobwhite quail are killed proportionate to the acreage hunted, not to mention proportionate to the expenses incurred raising them. A thousand-acre course on a ten-thousand-acre plantation is shot on an average of once every ten days. In a good year, thousands of birds are left at the end of the season, so when the boss decides to pack some into the freezer, the bounty hunters are called in.

To those who covet the opportunity to thin out a quail population I would suggest getting into the dog business, learning how to shoot really well, and preparing to kiss some demanding ass. To those who grind their teeth and make "Damn rich!" comments, all I can say is that these shooting plantations have been around for three quarters of a century or more. And although I don't pretend to know what motivates their owners, the bottom line is that they pour huge sums of money into both habitat improvements and research, which indirectly benefits quail and turkey nationwide. Bobwhites are immensely vulnerable to hunting pressure, and if these private preserves were opened to the public the quail population would be decimated in three years. I say that without criticism because the bird is so much fun to hunt, shoot, and eat, and it would be impossible to apply rules of decorum to hunters who haven't enjoyed decent shooting in twenty years. For obvious reasons, this quandary of private versus public access to hunting haunts the future of the sport.

Anyway, the brothers in question don't miss, and I don't mean that as a figure of speech. I mean: birds get up, birds fall down. They ride walking horses with greased gaits behind perfectly trained English pointers on grounds where the quail are pampered like bevies of high-priced models. I rode along because I had leased seven hundred acres of a plantation belonging to my cousins, which I hunted on foot. The undergrowth that year was ferocious, and the operator I had hired to mow the worst of it before hunting season was famous for his taste in cheap whiskey and taking naps, both of which he indulged the moment I left him alone. I can't say I blamed him. The cover, the heat, and the insects competed with memories of old movies produced in the jungles of Borneo. However there were quail everywhere: crossing the roads, flushing in front of the tractor, perched in trees, and whistling from inside the deep perplexity of untended Southern vegetation. It was, to say the least, frustrating not being able to get at them on foot. Therefore, with two weeks left in the season and only a handful of birds logged in the game book, I called the plantation's manager.

On a clear and cold February morning, the portcullis leading to this game-bird kingdom opened on one trailer full of dogs, another full of horses, the two brothers, the manager, and the owner's blessings.

The brothers were in their late twenties, fair-skinned, tough from running bird dogs 250 days a year, and polite as only Southerners know how to be. They were also very quick about saddling the horses, readying the guns, and getting dogs on the ground. They had brought four brace: seven English pointers and a thin-coated white setter with pink eyes. The dogs wore shock collars but were encouraged to hunt wide. They complemented each other and little if any cover escaped their solicitude.

Weather and habitat dictate the rhythm of any hunt,

but add to that the gait of a horse and you begin to understand why plantation quail-hunting is the sport of kings, or certainly of presidents. I have hunted on top of animals whose cadences have varied from somnolent oscillations to the consternation of slam-dancing, from horses that were eventually sold for dog food to slick-coated, small-headed, gaited horses from Tennessee and Mississippi. As with dogs, guns, and even women, you get what you pay for.

The objective is to blanket as much ground as the dogs can handle in a pattern that gridlocks the cover, an objective that varies depending on scenting conditions, ability of the dogs, and number of birds per acre. The course, therefore, is either hunted methodically or as quickly as possible. The rhythm of each hunt differs as a result of choices that grow instinctive with time. On any given day, I, like every other hunter, have worked hard and never seen a bird, dragged my heels the next, and killed my limit by lunch. A fundamental reason for hunting.

A decade ago, a friend and I leased six hundred of the sorriest, most treeless, weediest acres of central Florida on which lived thirty coveys of bobwhite quail. On opening day we killed the same number of birds as there were coveys. The land was a wild food factory that no one had hunted for three years. The course the brothers, the manager, and I hunted that February day was similar in that it was rough as a cob and full of birds. That day I was finally hunting the lease from the correct angle, which was high above the cover that had ripped my ass to shreds for three months.

The brothers used 20-gauge plugged automatics. They held the guns barrel up with the butt snug against their thighs, or scabbarded, stock forward for quick unsheathing. They shot one-handed from the saddle more accurately than 80 percent of all the shooters I have known shooting conventionally.

I knew the whereabouts of the first covey, which the dogs quickly found, having shot into it earlier in the year on a cold morning in January when the cover was thin and wet and pushed into the ground. I had found three coveys and shot four birds (already the best morning of the year) when Mabel, the English pointer, stole quietly up to point on the edge of a fallow field grown up in dog fennel. The covey was twenty feet beyond the bitch, fanned around the stump of a live oak tree whose roots had suckered and formed an umbrella that rattled as I walked through. The birds jumped straight up through the branches in my face and at eye level split into two separate directions across the open field. I shot twice, killing three birds with the right barrel and a fourth one with the second. Not only a novel approach to filling the icebox, but an oddity under any circumstances because I shoot a 28-gauge, and unprecedented in that all four birds were male bobwhite quail.

So, having done my share for that particular covey's parenthood planning, I declined to shoot. The brothers got off their horses and walked at top speed to and beyond the dogs. The covey got up, six shots rang out, six birds fell down, and the covey no longer existed. These boys were great killers and the most endearing men one would ever want to be with in the field. They love to hunt so much that every September they and two friends load their guns, dogs, ammo, junk food, and themselves in a Suburban after work on a Wednesday and drive nonstop from southern Georgia to Saskatchewan, Canada. They hunt Friday, Saturday, and Sunday, head the car south, and report back to work Wednesday morning. Their three-day bag usually exceeds one hundred Hungarian partridge and fifty or more sharp-tailed grouse.

The brothers work a tough six-day week that often includes cruising the swamp at night for lost dogs. They train dogs in the snake-riddled heat of summer and then guide the boss and his well-heeled guests during the fall and winter. Dogs and horses are fed, cleaned, trained, tended to when injured, and looked for when lost or running deer. The tack is lathered every night, the runs are washed, the stables mucked out, and the animals salved. The pressure of performing just right, six days a week for four and a half months, builds as the hunting season progresses. Admonishments from the mouths of Yankees, even politely understated, stick in the throats of Southerners, particularly when the smallest comment breeds uncertainty as to one's future.

A time warp of sorts enclosed my companions and me in an historical sporting bubble, impenetrable and mostly incomprehensible to the rest of the working world. We hunted from horseback behind the best dogs in the country on hills that rose and fell into a lake famous for its bass and for birds that fly as fast as model airplanes. The hands-in-the-pockets morning gave way to a sweet-smelling day with floods of sunshine slanted by the dreamy shimmer of a late-winter sky. If we had been loafers, we could have loafed to perfection, but we weren't.

We hunted from eight to noon and from two to five, the brothers shooting singles from horseback and the manager and I taking turns shooting covey rises from the ground. The horses moved through the woods quickly until contact between dog and quail was made. Then we hunted carefully, leaving a few birds in each covey but, to be honest, not keeping count. Good shooters don't miss the first shot, and the brothers rarely did. They assured the first birds, caught up with the second, and once in a while stretched out for a third. One shoots for food, for the love of killing, or for making the shot; the brothers shot for all three.

That night I slipped the feathered bodies of seventy-nine bobwhite quail into baggies, froze them, and sent care packages all over the country to people I knew liked them. The dogs pointed nineteen coveys—thirteen held for the guns—and singles were shot from four of the six coveys that wild-flushed. It was a day I think about, a day in hell for Mr. Bob, a day that in some ways I regret, but also a day spent with two young men whose naive enthusiasm reminded me of myself twenty years ago; the puzzle was and still is my absence of guilt.

I did not renew the lease the following year but heard from the plantation manager that the hunting was as good as ever. So much for my after-the-fact population concerns, or rather, this is a good example of how privately managed land fares against land that is pounded on a daily basis. The birds that survived that one-day war regrouped and went on about picking partners for the breeding season. Had those same birds been hit two or three times a week for an entire season, none would have survived.

★   ★   ★

When I hunt I position myself firmly back in the food chain as a predator, and a good one because of my range. Shooting used to be a natural act for me, from the eyes to the hands, but now that I am not as sharp the act has gone from the eyes to the mind, back to the eyes, and finally to the finger that pulls the trigger. The added wrinkle has slowed me down. Thinking and shooting don't mix, and my style, which used to be instinctive, has become more mechanical. To aggravate the problem, although I look for the easy shots they don't interest me, and instead of assuring them I miss them out of momentary ennui. The longer I see the target, the more likely I am to miss. Quail shooting is the paramount remedy for shooting nerves, something I still catch the first week of the season but get over when I adhere to either of these extremes in social advice: "When the birds get up, if you chew tobacco, spit over your shoulder before you shoot" and "A gentleman may be in haste, but he should never be in a hurry." The bobwhites of the Southern woods, as opposed to the quail of the open country of southern Texas, are excellent targets, particularly if one thinks in terms of doubles. Frank Forester summed them up quite nicely 150 years ago: "The Virginia quail is probably the hardest bird in the world to kill quickly, cleanly, and certainly."

On researching the bobwhite quail I came upon hundreds of records kept for posterity, or was it glory? The best recorded shooting was in Lynchburg, Virginia, in 1851, when three gentlemen shot more than one hundred quail apiece in a day's hunting. In the same year in Rock Island, Mississippi, four hundred quail were netted in one afternoon and shipped to New York, where they sold for a dollar a dozen. A few years later, in "The Spirit of the Times," a letter from Iowa Territory mentioned that the correspondent had netted ten thousand quail in one season. A man hunting with his dog on foot in eastern Louisiana in 1889 shot ninety-two rounds, with which he killed and found eighty-three bobwhite quail. Undoubtedly, one of the brothers' ancestors.

IV

Now that I recognize cruelty for what it is, the more I see it, the more ashamed I am of my own. When I feel the life flow out of the breast of a crippled bird, I wonder about the sanity of what I'm doing and don't have an answer. I think about it and go on, just as I think about the children I could save by paying for their medical care, or the homeless, or the elderly, but I don't help them either, and, except when I am faced with a bird I have wounded, go on about my life blissfully.

Inherent cruelty of the kind that is demoralizing to a conscientious hunter is fatwood on the fires of those who want to see the sport abolished. It is killing for no reason, killing for the numbers and losing cripples for lack of looking.

Nowadays, I kill only what I intend to eat or give away, but in the process of hunting I can and do conjure nightmarish visions of birds in pain, of birds grimly waiting to die because I have broken something as necessary to them as a wing.

Because physical pain has occupied an intimate place in my life I hate to cripple, and the more sophisticated the nervous system of a species the less inclined I am to hunt it. No one really knows what makes men act as if they didn't know better, but I warrant to say there isn't a hunter in the entire history of hunting who hasn't at one time or another killed for no reason, targeted an animal to test his marksmanship, forgotten it, and left it behind. In my case shame invariably followed.

Indoctrinated to believe that nature is servant to man, that we alone are endowed with a soul, and that beasts have no feelings, we have conveniently pushed nature and its lower forms of life to the bottom of our list of priorities. Though the deformities we as hunters inflict on the natural world are minuscule in the light of the festering and permanent sores picked by the political machinations of business, they nevertheless pour out of the same faucet as dominion, arrogance, and dead-on stupidity. The truly fortunate hunters are those like B. J. Pruit, who never give death a second thought, who don't feel remorse or empathy for a crippled bird, a gut-shot deer, a steel-trapped fox. Mention mother and country and tears swell, but not for the wood duck that fell too far away to bother with. They are the fortunate ones, for not having to carry the weight of that broken wing on their souls. Unfortunately for the sport, there have been too many "fortunate ones," and their pervasive callousness has not only spread but has tainted the rest of us who, for better or worse, at the very least think about what we do or have done. We are a minority in a rapidly decaying sport.

I do not delude myself: my motives for providing bobwhite quail with food and cover are self-serving because for three months each fall and winter I shoot and eat them. It also happens that when hunting season arrives I think of them as my birds, to be shared with whom I choose, when I choose. That is not at all in keeping with how I felt as a young man growing up in southern Florida where, as a part-time poacher, I was not only irreverent of posted signs but firmly believed that land belonged to everyone; I took pleasure in hunting game others claimed as theirs. Those were the sweaty, muddy days of hunting private land, of outfoxing foremen, and of making myself and my dog small under the palmetto bush while the Fish and Game helicopter hung overhead, tempting, like a decoying duck. It was also a decade to be young, a time of hard-ons and loud laughter, of middle fingers permanently raised at the establishment, in pursuit of everything except wisdom at a time when there were half as many people in the world. In the book of Daniel it says "They shall drive you [King Nebuchadnezzar] from among men, and thy dwelling shall be with the beasts of the field." To be drenched in the dew of heaven and to grow the feathers of eagles sounds like a pretty good place to be driven to these days, given the alternatives.

Thirty years later, the positions are reversed. I invite the game wardens to sit and wait on my land until someone is stupid enough to shoot at the plastic white-tailed deer decoy, complete with glowing red eyes, planted in the open field across the county road from the farm. One man got caught twice in so many years. He paid his fine, lost his rifle, and six months later shot the same piece of plastic, in the same place, with a different gun and said "Durn!" when they cuffed him. I'm betting that he'll be back.

V

By the middle of January in Tallahassee, when the natural and planted food is turning into compost, I supplement my quails' diet with cracked corn or milo—milo is cheaper and doesn't sour as quickly—in twenty or so feeders set in good cover throughout the farm. This feeds the cotton rats, as well as adding fat to my birds' diminishing body weights. If nighttime temperatures drop below freezing for more than a few days, I broadcast grain from an electric spreader on the tailgate of the truck in those places I have seen or heard coveys, or where I have shot birds that feel light in the hand. Many of the plantations rotate food on the courses they are going to hunt, accomplishing both an additional source of energy and a concentration of birds for the dogs to find. This path of life and death is known as the honey trail. One might argue the morality behind drawing birds to food to better shoot them, but such has been the custom since man baited hooks and hurled spears. On the other hand, if one thinks of sport as carrying certain moral obligation, or the evolution of man's principles, the ethicality of the honey trail is debatable.

There is no question in my mind that the most valuable work being performed in wildlife management today involves telemetry, a relatively new science, expensive because it requires a substantial investment in man-hours but so diversified in its applications that transmitters have been implanted in species ranging from rattlesnakes to adulterers.

Bobwhite quail have been, and still are, one of the most studied game birds in the world, and now that the logistics of making and attaching transmitters is perfected, the data that are being gathered establish habitat use, feeding patterns, and mortality due to weather, illness, and predation, including the gun. Telemetry is also in the process of disavowing many of the allegations about bobwhite quail we all grew up with.

"There is no such thing as an unproductive point," says Ted Devoes, an open-faced, sunburned young man working toward his doctorate in game management from Auburn University on a three-year quail project at Pinneland Plantation south of Albany, Georgia. In his first season he outfitted 140 quail with transmitters and banded an additional 350. I hunted Pinneland with its owner, Prosser Mellon, for two days late in the winter of 1993, escorted by a mounted retinue of scientists wearing earphones and carrying radar an-

tennae. Others rode along while musing over biological matters and offering their expertise in all aspects of the piney
woods from turkey hunting to stressed-out pine plantations.
We hunters went on about the business of hunting as if the
entourage weren't there. Devoes and his assistant had been
monitoring quail in four one-thousand-acre tracts for a year,
banding birds at night, following specific coveys in every
conceivable weather, retrieving the remains of dead birds,
and, from the markings and scratches on the plastic-coated
transmitters, identifying the varied causes of death. A little
like a U.N. delegation, Ted and his helper had monitored
every hunt on the assigned tracts since the beginning of the
season and knew the whereabouts of every single bobwhite
quail. We nimrods didn't know dick, except when the dogs
pointed.

The first afternoon we moved eighteen coveys. An
incredible number under any circumstances, made more incredible because this was the final week of the hunting season,
and even more surprising because the last time I had shot at
Pinneland (two years earlier) the plantation was averaging
thirteen coveys a day. I learned that of the three factors that
had made a difference, one was achieved through management, one by Prosser Mellon, and one by God. In the first
place, the woods had been seriously opened to the sun, twice
as many food plots had been sown into the habitat, and the
serious figure of two million new bicolor Lespedeza seedlings
over ten thousand acres had been planted. Secondly, Prosser
Mellon, a quiet man who hides a wry sense of humor behind
a somewhat convenient hearing disorder, had finally discouraged his British-born game hog of a stepfather from in-

viting his murdering cronies by enhancing their daily libations with enough Ex-Lax to make the old boys yearn for the comfort of their men's club in London. Prosser's bold administration effectively cut the hunting days on Pinneland by a half. Thirdly, the 1992–1993 breeding season had been graced with the perfect amount of summer rains and an unusual percentage of late hatches. There were birds everywhere, sometimes as many as three coveys in the air at one time.

The year-end statistics demonstrated the following: Fifteen percent of the hens raised two broods, presumably leaving the cock bird with the chore of raising the first hatch to adulthood. This information alone disclaims previous belief that hens only renest if disturbed or after losing eggs of young ones to weather or predation. It appears that on Pinneland, anyway, such is not the case; when during the evening report I suggested that perhaps Mellon raised sexually deviant quail, I was told to shut up.

Bobwhites are territorial and studies on birds outfitted with transmitters the size of fingernails confirm that individual coveys claim specific real estate. Devoes, who is also a bird hunter, advances a somewhat tongue-in-cheek example of the reluctance of quail to fly out of their home range. He theorizes that the covey a hunter flushes and observes making a right-angle turn at the limits of his vision is not attempting an escape maneuver as much as it is trying to remain inside the boundary of its territory, a territory the covey is intimately familiar with, from its gopher holes to its severed treetops.

It was also established that on any given day of the hunting season the Pinneland bird dogs—and these are very good dogs—find 30 percent of the available coveys. Of those coveys pointed but not shot, 41 percent wild-flushed and 59 percent ran. The latter figure is higher than anyone ever dreamed, particularly since it occurred in good piney cover. From that statistic came Ted Devoes' statement "There is no such thing as an unproductive point." A good dog points the scent of a covey; what that covey does in terms of running away does not diminish the dog's original contact.

Prosser and I are pretty quick getting off our horse and honoring a point (he is also an exceptional shot). We walk quickly to either side of the dogs and keep moving until the birds get up. That is as it should be when quail hunting, but twice that afternoon we followed dogs pointing and relocating coveys for hundreds of yards before birds began getting up. It would seem that these princely little American birds have over the years genetically adapted themselves to become the roadrunners of the East.

When we were unsuccessful in flushing a pointed covey and the dogs had been sent off to find a new one, my curiosity would get the better of me and I would ask Devoes where the birds had been. Sometimes he would point to a food patch a quarter of a mile away; other times he would grin and point to a shrub sixty feet from where we had hunted. Ted knew more than the dogs, the handlers, and the shooters. He was a black belt in twenty-first-century electronic wildlife research.

However the main problem with research on these beautiful Southern plantations—telemetric or otherwise—is that these are mollycoddled birds. While a percentage of the data is valid, quail that live on public hunting grounds or on

unmanaged private property are not going to enjoy the benefits, health-wise or otherwise, that these blue-blooded birds
do, and while most plantation owners are careful not to over-
shoot a course or shoot down a covey, such is not the case on
public hunting grounds. One could argue then that Buckner's
theory on quail losses in early hatches would not hold up if 15
percent of the females raised two broods. But I prefer to believe, until the data prove me wrong, that just as with humans, pampered quail eating the equivalent of caviar for
breakfast are going to behave like wealthy women and divorce accordingly.

One of the most extensive studies on poor man's
quail was made on the 150,000-acre base at Fort Bragg in
North Carolina, where the soil is rank and the hunting pressure heavy. The harvest of bobwhite quail went from approx-
imately 8,000 birds a year in 1970 to 650 in 1985. The
seven-year telemetry study indicated the following: A 60 percent raptor-kill in late winter for lack of cover, continuous
dispersal of the coveys by hunters, who took an additional 20
percent of the birds, and a mammalian predation rate of 20
percent; quail survival rates averaged 6 percent over four years
at Fort Bragg as opposed to 25 percent at Tall Timber Research Station near Tallahassee, where the birds are well cared
for. The food plots at Fort Bragg had been planted haphaz-
ardly, with little or no escape cover, inviting all sorts of predators, including hunters, to a concentration of targets with
nowhere to go. Late-winter hunting had the effect of diminishing the breeding stock, both through direct harvest of birds
that had survived the winter as well as by scattering bobwhites

at the peak of the accipiter conventions. This study reinforces the feeling that we are no longer dealing with a compensatory harvest—killing birds that would have died anyway—but an additive harvest: a harvest of birds that might otherwise have survived to reproduce, particularly when numbers are down and the cover is poor.

The recommendations that have surfaced from the various telemetry studies being held across the country are: One, that no more than one-third of a covey should be shot, including cripples. Two, that food plots should be located as close to cover as possible. Three, that the hunting season should be shortened (particularly in the South) so that it doesn't dovetail into a migration of talons. And four, that one should avoid shooting coveys just before dark, as they won't have time to regroup and will spend a long and vulnerable night pursued by living nightmares shaped like owls and foxes.

Forget the studies made in Texas—unless you are from that state—because management is secondary to rain. Droughts are always destructive to the feathered race, and that applies in the Lone Star State; on the other hand the right amount of rain in southern Texas spells more quail per acre than all the rest of the states added together.

It is theorized, through observation at Fort Bragg, that hawks respond to gunfire in a Pavlovian manner and fly to the sound looking for an easy meal. Telemetry has also proven that about half the hunted bobwhite quail run for dear life on or about the third time they hear the bells or electronic beepers worn by bird dogs, not to mention the cavalry of horses, mule-pulled wagons, and general jibber-jabber. Poachers have moved silently through the woods for centuries for a reason, and birds hear as well as game wardens, probably better.

VI

When it comes to cooking the game the French and Italians have so little left of, they are the masters. Growing up in a village in Normandy, I ate wild animals in the homes of farmers, plumbers, carpenters, grocery-store owners, the bourgeois, and off Sevres-ware from castles whose owners invited me, once in a while, to shoot driven birds.

Game was habitually served once or twice a week during the five-month-long French hunting season, and from those thousands of homes—in which birds and boar and rabbits were roasted, braised, and fried—emerged over the centuries a deep appreciation for and understanding of the taste of animals that live in the wild, of forest fragrances, and an innumerable number of recipes with which to cook them. One can only wish that the French and Italians hadn't been such pigs when it came to the slaughter of what they excel at preparing. The fact that game is generally poorly cooked in the United States and that the majority of the population doesn't have a taste for it is, with hindsight, a godsend.

A la pointe du fusil means at the tip of the gun, and implies freshly killed game. *Faisandé* means pheasanted (if that were a word) and suggests game that is hung until the germs of its intestines invade the balance of its tissues, decomposing and softening them while strengthening the fundamental taste of the meat, which in the case of pheasants, wild turkey, and quail is bland. Three days on the gallows will relax muscles and fibers as surely as the sun loosens the reserve of young women, allowing the wild flavor of its nature and the environment it lived in to be released.

I hang birds, in the case of ungutted quail, for three days (longer for drawn birds) in the bottom third of a refrigerator or, weather permitting, on a breezy porch. If, after that time, the quail are not eaten, I freeze them in full feathers in a zip-lock plastic bag designed for other things. When the bird is thawed, the feathers pluck effortlessly and the innards surface in a tight, hard ball, ready for the disposal. The drawback to this method of freezing is that one loses the use of the bird's liver, which after dangling in mid-stomach for three days has matured beyond consumption; the heart and gizzard are fine and should be used in the stock or stuffing for added taste. Brillat-Savarin, author of *The Physiology of Taste,* wrote that "game likes to be waited on like a pension from the government to a man of letters who never learned how to flatter." I once ate a mallard duck that had been hung for seventeen days. Taking things too far used to be a habit of mine; in that particular case, a bad one.

Hanging quail drawn or undrawn is matter of preference. I opt for the latter, so long as the bird isn't gut-shot—a gamble that leaves me open to no less odorous surprises, in these abysmal days of infected pursuits, as any other grail, confirming my fears that the past held more promise than the present. Medically speaking, hung meat carries its asides, gout being one of them. But then, there are so many things one shouldn't do, for the same explicit closeness of quarters, that as long as one is fully prepared for a surprise, why not indulge a little?

The sooner a freshly killed quail is introduced to the skillet or the oven, the better. The bird's bruised flesh must not be allowed to gather itself around tendons and bones because, short of a slow rewarming of the muscles inside of which the bird's flavor is in retreat, the quail will be almost tasteless.

Bobwhite can be delicious slow-cooked, depending on what puddle of liquid they are cooked in. If it is a can of noodle soup, the birds might as well be pen-raised; both flavors deserve each other. On the other hand, I have braised quail next to shallots, small carrots, duck thighs, peaches, reduced veal stock, and port, and the dish was so good I took risks and licked the casserole before sending it to the bottom of the sink. I have also cooked quail in white wine on a bed of seedless grapes and wild green onion, atop a slice of bread. I have poached them in gumbo seconds ahead of the shrimp, and substituted them for gray partridge in the famous *Perdrix au choux,* substituting collard greens for the cabbage and adding balsamic pepper vinegar before serving. These dishes take twenty-five minutes of cooking in low, wet heat instead of twelve minutes in a hot oven.

However, given my druthers I pick my quail, brown them in a skillet with butter (which also plumps them up nicely), and roast them quickly at high heat. Skinning birds (unless there is not enough left to deal with) is an insult to one's palate as well as to the bird whose life one has terminated. I view skinning birds with the same critical eye I reserve for those who cook their meals inside plastic pouches—a desolate habit of those who can only be described as the premature ejaculators of the culinary nineties.

If one cuts the wings off a quail it becomes a candidate for rolling on the grill. Quail are built to roll, and as long as they are basted and tended to, they are exquisite this way. In the South the tendency is to split the birds up the backbone and flatten them so they look like bats. In either case, the leeway for making mistakes on the grill is minimal. The hot cooking surface draws the moisture from the bird, so when the quail is ready a prompt sitting of the guests at the table is mandatory; three minutes on the wrong side of perfect and the birds are fit for playing Ping-Pong, but not for eating.

In the long run, sleep endures better than food and food better than sex, a matter of wearying innards. It is with a certain nostalgia that I remember a time almost twenty years ago when I could demoralize a leg of lamb by myself; now I gnaw the meat off a shank and call it a night. This waning of my carnal appetites, however, has not diminished my enthusiasm for quality, and for that reason my favorite person to cook for is me. With no criticism, pressure, advice, queries, or demands leveled against me, I am for a few precious moments master of my destiny. I choose the ingredients, the method, the timing, the accompaniments, the presentation, and when and where to savor my creation. When what I cook is not to my satisfaction, I throw it across the room without raising anyone's eyebrow; when it's good, I boast of my exploits and the dogs nod their approval.

These days, if I squeeze the trigger I squeeze it at something that flies, and if I hit it, I eat it. I keep, for that reason, a spaniel at heel (or thereabouts) to deliver the bird, whose funeral I wish to celebrate in my stomach, not in that of a raccoon. In the case of quail, eating one is a delight that, coupled with the right hanging time, is like kissing a young girl, a soft-skinned beauty not altogether attuned to the practical matters of hygiene, but lovely all the same. Lolita at daybreak comes to mind.

Five dressed bobwhite quail weigh about a pound. I know a Cajun who regularly eats that many, fried, in one sitting, but he is *un peu touché,* as they say over there. I have had a few deep-fried quail that melted in my mouth, but what I remember most about the others is the grease on my shirt and an intense desire to brush my teeth. In the same vein, the charm of eating barbecued quail, usually bacon-wrapped, in the fields during a break in the shooting action is somewhat diminished when what appears on the platter looks like a cluster of frogs fished out of an incinerator. The habit of wrapping bacon around quail is fine if one likes bacon, because that is what the bird will taste like: smoked pig. Salt pork or fatback, blanched to lessen the salt content, makes for a neutral substitute. Most of the time, quail and doves that should be delicious lie on the plate like an insult. Subtlety isn't the driving force behind Southern cooking.

Now that I have insulted all those in need of insults—as well as others who aren't—I will offer some alternatives to criticism.

The subtleties and individuality of a bobwhite quail depend on what the bird is stuffed with and what it sits on. Beginning with the latter, the birds can sit on a julienne of vegetables, an apple round (baked longer than the ten to twelve minutes required for the birds), a purée of just about anything from chestnuts to garlic mashed potatoes, thin corn crepes or fried squares of polenta, grits, etc. The flavors should be delicate; therefore forget smoked sausages, Mexican bean dip, and Gouda cheese, as that is what you will taste. A gracious Southern lady stuffs her quail with oysters; a French one with ratatouille. I like to parboil sweetbreads, pull them into chunks half the size of my thumb, powder them with flour, and sauté them at very high heat for thirty seconds before pushing them into the bird's stomach. Sometimes, when making crepes from corn, a vegetable that marries well with bobwhites, I undercook some of the batter in the same buttered skillet I browned the birds in and stuff the corn mush into the birds before sending them to the oven. A duxelles of mushrooms (a good one made with morels or cèpes is advised) is at home both inside the bird or on a square of fried toast. Last winter I added fresh lump-meat crab to the duxelles and licked my chops.

I have roasted quail with everything from shallots to pitted grapes, cherries, calf brains, white *boudin*, browned apple slices—but always elements that are neutral enough to allow the subtle flavor of the bird to prevail. For those who like rice, fill a quail with risotto; for those who like sweet things, spoon in some yams; for those who enjoy expensive experiments, shove a black truffle up its ass. My favorite quail mattress is one made with foie gras; my favorite baste, the dewy sweat of a pom-pom-twirling cheerleader.

A classic French stuffing for game birds (say eight quail) is made with half a pound of washed chicken livers (duck is better if you can get them), one-quarter pound of somewhat fatty pork, two cloves of garlic, two shallots, a spoonful of cognac (Madeira or port will work), a pinch of fresh thyme, a handful of dry bread crumbs, a spoonful of flour, salt, pepper, two eggs, and the heart, liver, and gizzards of the birds. Transfer the ingredients into a blender and let her rip for a minute. The stuffing should be thick and moist. Needless to say, more or less ingredients can be added: paprika, leeks, dog tongues, etc.

Last time I was in France, I asked Richard Labbé, a twenty-six-year-old chef with twelve years of schooling and salaried experience already behind him, to make something so delicious and complicated no one in America would ever try to duplicate it; the bobwhites were domesticated, the meal was not.

Eight quail were partially deboned from the inside, leaving the legs intact, by first removing the wishbone between the chest and the neck and then, using a small knife, working the blade between the bird's ribs and skin upward to the keel. Using his fingers, Labbé patiently pulled and cut the meat away from the tiny bones until the entire rib cage lay on the kitchen table and the birds lay deflated, see *despondent*. Labbé cut two large truffles into thin slices and slipped as many as he could fit between the quail's breast meat and skin. He filled the boned cavity with the classic stuffing, using instead of pork, which he too feels imparts an unhealthy flavor to the delicate nature of the dish, the meat of two additional quail. But as he said, he could just as well have used a little thigh meat from a chicken or duck, or even a peeled apple. Finally he inserted an additional finger of fresh foie gras in the middle of the stuffing and sealed the cavity by trussing the birds with kitchen string.

The quail were browned in clarified butter, removed from the cast-iron pot, and replaced with chopped onions, carrots, a sprig of thyme, and a small laurel leaf. He simmered the *mirepoix* until the vegetables were soft, reinstated the birds, flamed them with two shots of cognac, and moved the cocotte, uncovered, to the middle of the oven (350 degrees) for ten minutes. While the birds were cooking he reduced two cups of veal stock down to one and added salt, pepper, and a spoonful of flour dissolved in white wine to bind the stock. When the ten minutes were up, he added the reduced veal stock to the quail until the birds were bathing in sauce, covered the pot, and put it back into the oven for ten minutes more. During the cooking of the quail he decrusted eight pieces of white bread and fried them in clarified butter until they turned color. Lastly he removed the lid, basted the birds with the cooking liquid, and roasted them for five more minutes.

Labbé tested the birds by inserting a cooking needle into a quail breast and touching it to his tongue. Satisfied that the temperature of the needle was as it should be, he moved the birds to a platter, covered them with foil, and rested them on the opened oven door while he reduced the sauce, strained and threw out the vegetables, added more truffles, topped the pieces of toast with a slice of foie gras, and, moments before serving the dish, whisked off-heat a tablespoon of butter into the saucepan. He explained that the birds could wait, covered, on the apron of the oven for up to twenty minutes, but that one should never bring the sauce back to a boil once the butter had been added. He said that cooking, like painting, requires layers of thought and ingredients, a search for the right colors, textures, and affirmation. Good cooking, particularly of foods that involve intricate flavors, equals lots of dishes to wash.

The quail were presented sitting on their individual foie gras toasts next to a mountain of French string beans and an excess of thinner french fries, all under the supporting presence of a magnum of Château Canon 1975.

VII

The future of both public and private bobwhite quail hunting will one day flow out of aviaries. There isn't much public land left in the South and where there is, there aren't enough funds to raise and manage the numbers of wild birds needed to satisfy the thousands of hunters who have nowhere else to hunt. Take it from someone who checks out every deal, reads the daily ads in the local mullet wrapper (newspaper), compares prices on secondhand machinery, and buys the cheapest fertilizer and last year's seeds: raising wild quail in this final decade of the twentieth century is very expensive. The slightest hiccup in weather, an unscheduled predator fly-in, a pack of wild dogs, or a handful of tabby cats will upset a bobwhite population whose success as a species is dubious to begin with. At best, one hundred eggs will produce fifty chicks, of which twelve will see fall and seven live to breed. Raising wild quail with a less-than-full wallet is not viable in terms of effort versus returns. Even if I manage my eight-hundred-acre farm correctly, the weather is favorable, and I raise thirty coveys a year, all it would take to wipe out that population (or at least push it over the neighbor's fence) is a friend who can shoot, half a dozen good bird dogs, a death wish, and two weeks' time. Last season the total bag for the farm was sixty-one bobwhites, fewer than the brothers and I shot in one day.

Simply put, the acreage and management required to build enough coveys to hunt two or three times a week for three and a half months is available only to the wealthiest of hunters. The future of those others who want to work dogs and shoot bobwhites rests in releasing pen-raised birds on small tracts of land, or sinking into the trough of low-rent commercial bird farms—the put-out-in-the-morning, kill-before-lunch, pay-and-move-on slaughterhouses.

For me to criticize this inevitable trend would be presumptuous and insulting, so I won't, except to suggest that these birds are merely living targets, released in the wild for the sole reason of being shot, and have nothing to do with the intrinsic act of hunting. However, just because I would rather suck my thumb than shoot pen-raised birds doesn't mean that others less fortunate than I shouldn't take advantage of what is left of an old tradition.

The practice of releasing bobwhites (chickens: thousands on some plantations) on the ground before the beginning of the hunting season makes for a better flying bird but is considerably more expensive than releasing fewer quail, or even the exact number requested moments before the shooting party takes to the woods. Some of the better pen-raised birds I know are released in early September for a mid-October to mid-March cull. Gillionville Plantation, outside of Albany, Georgia, offers, on its eight thousand acres, hunting from horseback and mule-drawn wagons, lodging in an exquisite antebellum house, and a quality of food and service the most persnickety of sportsmen could wish for. The owner expects that 40 percent of the eight thousand quail (one per acre) put out in August will die in the first two weeks after their release, 20 percent of the remaining stock before the season opens. The birds that survive to sing Christmas carols fly well, well enough to fool most modern hunters into thinking they are shooting wild birds. An assumption to be cherished until the dazzling day they are introduced to the real thing.

The worst-case scenario is the game factory that puts out the quail while the shooter is readying his accoutrement. Birds that once pointed usually have to be booted into flight by the shooter or dog handler; birds that wobble into the first thicket have been known to die of a heart attack on the re-flush. The common denominator in all quail management is money. An afternoon of shooting wobblers on a specific fifty-acre allotment of land, with B. J. Pruit and friends, on a preserve that kills between eighty and one hundred thousand quail a year (!), or a week of living the antebellum life, while not as expensive as raising wild birds, will nevertheless stretch a man's pocketbook.

The good news is that there are a handful of bird

farms in the South that have had the foresight to raise quail in large aviaries. One man raises his birds in a gutted motel with minimal human contact and trained dogs that romp through the bedrooms once a day to acquaint the birds with predation and the usefulness of their wings. These quail are released in the wild at night, in small numbers, next to food and cover. Their survival rate is considerably higher, as is their value as targets, and a small percentage live to mate in the wild.

To those quail hunters who will in the years to come forgo the wilderness experience for a tamer venue and the companionship of their peers, bobwhites, like pheasants, are the answer. Pen-raised birds lend themselves well to the sham of not-so-highly-strung bird dogs, older horses, mules with domino-size teeth, German guns, young whiskey, fast food, and good-natured lies. The only thing really missing from the older scenario is the bird itself: the wild *Colinus virginianus,* the miniature icon of the American game bird, a little bird with a long history. However, like all shades of ignorance, the real thing won't be missed by those who don't know any better. Hunters will momentarily enter a setting totally foreign to their daily lives, a setting that will remind them of their child-hood or a book they read, and be absolutely blissful at the opportunity to draw a bead on a small brown bird with ab-normally long shinbones. Better yet they will actually kill some, unaware that, like the men who hunt them, the birds fly at a leisurely pace.

One of the most important factors in deciding whether to raise wild or pen-raised bobwhites (or any kind of game bird) is how to deal with predation. Does one go to war against raccoons, skunks, possums, dogs, cats, et al., or does one flow with the natural process, knowing that the added numbers of quail are going to attract an added number of predators?

What is not voiced aloud but is known by everyone in the business is that the most damaging predation to bobwhite quail—70 percent—is avian in nature, specifically from the accipiter hawks. At the Tall Timber Research Station the highest quail count goes back to 1973, a year when the hawks were absent, a DDT kind of year. Federally protected, secretive, and quick, the blue darters, as they are called down here, are powered by short, broad wings to better elude the branches of the trees they hunt under. I catch shadowy glimpses of them during their northern migration about the same time the robins show up—which unfortunately for my quail is soon after burning—and again in the fall when the leaves are falling, the cover is stunted, and the understory revealed.

The increase in mammalian predators has been caused in part by the economic and social pressures on trapping. Foxes, raccoons, and the rest of the fur-bearing mammals have exploded back into hungry numbers.

A hundred years ago or even less, the best quail-hunting grounds were found next to small—one- or two-acre—quilts of diversified crops planted by tenants and small farmers. Those tenants ate the opossums, trapped the raccoons and foxes for money, and shot the chicken hawks. The worst-kept secret in quail management these days is that most local plantations and private shooting grounds habitually break the federal laws that protect the birds of prey, and quite honestly they have the most quail. The problem with all this killing for the benefit of one species over another is that it doesn't make moral sense; when it applies to humans it is considered an abomination. Our continuous meddling has imposed on nature the attitude of a plane whose wings have stalled and entered a spin. Pilots are taught that when everything fails, release the controls and the plane will right itself; it will right itself because it is designed to right itself, and inherently wants to do so. So does nature. This year, the accipiters ate me out of house and home in terms of quail. To a hawk I am a cheap supplier of fine foods. This year the Cooper's hawks came and went with the robins, and I would not trade either for a quail.

VIII

The toughest ticket in town is an invitation to shoot bobwhite quail on a private plantation. Exemptions include the local doctors, politicians, and lawyers, all of whom have historically profited from being needed commodities.

As a rule, though, bobwhite quail, ducks, and wild turkey are the sole property of the plantation owners who, to fend off unmitigated loneliness—not to mention boredom—invite out-of-town friends to hunt the birds that were so assiduously tended to for nine long months. The end of a week of shooting finds one group of tweed-clad sportsmen nudged out the door in favor of a fresh set of faces, en route on Victor airways, from colder regions and countries. Friends and friends of friends crisscross each other in the sky, mansions overflow with friendly pink faces, domestics put in double-time to make up for the dog days of summer, and the evenings brim with synergetic, political, and artistic babble, crossword puzzles and parlor games with nary a difference of opinion. Guests are expected to be entertaining, if not via their fowling abilities, certainly through the correctness of their politics, social graces, business acumen, and general good-fellowship. For example, talking through one's teeth is recognized, braying is not; Yale is desirable, Harvard too liberal; Reagan equals God, Clinton *caca;* so forth and so on.

When I first moved to Tallahassee I was invited to hunt in a setting that elevated the word *beautiful* to heights I had never dreamed existed. There is, in everyone's mind's eye, a vision of perfection; for me it was northern Florida, early in December, before the golden landscape had buried itself. I hunted on rolling land that never ended, across fawn-colored fields anchored to expanses of red clay that reminded me of Africa, next to ponds and lakes onto which thousands of waterfowl showered daily, and under the shadowy limbs of huge trees that conjured the complicated words and feelings of the South. It was a game paradise, the likes of which I had not experienced since Sehoy Plantation in Union Springs, Alabama, twenty years before. Everything was mysterious and new and the dogs ran collarless and big across the broom sedge. The points were called by either a tall black man who went under the name of Two Man or his flanker, Lonnie, whose mare could outrun a deer. Lonnie would stand his ground, careful not to spook the pointed covey, and raise his hat high above his head for Two Man to see. I remember riding up at a full gallop, dismounting on the fly, walking with a beating heart beyond where the dogs made their stand, and shooting into the rising birds as if it were the most important thing in my life.

A decade has passed and my heart doesn't race for quail anymore. I love them, but I know just about everything there is to know about them and that takes its toll. Now I hunt to distance myself from the presumptuousness of life and to enlarge the peripheries of my estate. Perhaps this is what happens to men when they grow older, because when I was young I would envy my neighbor's shots and be annoyed over my missed ones. I would take questionable shots for the sake of making memorable ones, and keep shooting knowing full well I would lose more birds than I'd find. The list of my stupid behaviors is embarrassingly long, so now that I have lost most of the arrogance that breeds delusions and have given these matters a little more thought, I can only hope that just like an old whore I'll make a good wife and finish my life a better hunter.

Now that I know how to provide for quail and what it takes to improve their habitat in terms of both money and labor, when I hunt a new place I know how much of each has gone into the production. I look at the land as I would a piece of meat to be trimmed for the table, and in many ways that is sad, because I have lost the awe and wonder of innocence. The fairy-tale beauty of riding through the Southern pine-woods is tinged with critical curiosity, and in many ways that also is sad, in the same fashion as a moviemaker or a writer who watches or reads no longer for pleasure but to study the methods used by his peers.

IX

That plantations aren't managing for quail but managing for bird dogs is a statement I hear from many biologists, referring to the preseason mowing down of heavy cover. Some plantations take this to extremes by running a Bush Hog every fifty feet or so and then cross-mowing so that the undergrowth looks like a giant checkerboard. While I acknowledge that some plantation owners fart higher than their asses, in this case the fact that they want to watch their dogs work and at the same time ease the hardships of plowing through heavy cover for their friends, many of whom are old and out of shape, seems perfectly normal to me, particularly as the removal of cover is amply made up for by the quantity of food these quail would not otherwise enjoy.

In any event, who can blame a man for wanting to see his dogs work in a setting that is artificially inseminated to begin with? If killing is the real object, one should consider sending young men into the field in lieu of dogs, young biologists armed with maps, earphones, and telemetry equipment, and be done with it.

To rely on the financially fortunate to look after the well-being of the bobwhite quail population presents some problems; problems generated by the limitless availability of money, blue blood, new blood, and self-indulgence. It is a situation I understand for being raised under that mantle. It was not atypical for me to shoot in France and Scotland, New England, Florida and Alabama in one season; a good year perhaps, but not so unusual as to be catalogued as special. I am amazed, looking back forty years, at how much hunting and fishing I have done and how much of it I've forgotten or tucked away in some mildewed and somewhat embarrassed recess of my brain. And therein lies one of the fundamental problems of men and women of means who readily assume that the real world is the one they live in, rather than being forever grateful that their world is an exceptional domain that only a minuscule percentage of humanity can even imagine, much less understand. In the case of stewardship, indulgence is paid for by those who benefit from its perpetuity. This suggests that the motivation behind a well-managed quail program is not always the quantity of quail produced for the posterity of the species but the number produced compared to the neighbor. Good management practices with social overtones.

★   ★   ★

The generation before mine hunted big game in Africa, I hunted birds in Europe and North America, this generation hunts in Central and South America; God only knows where the next generation will be shooting. But one thing is certain: they will have to be wealthy to do so. The prices that are being paid early in this decade are already out of control: two and a half days of wild bobwhite quail hunting at a top ranch in southern Texas costs $3,000 a man, $2,000 to kill a white-tailed deer, $450 a turkey, and $16 a bird if one wants to shoot live-boxed pigeons. Needless to say, 80 percent of the guests wear the perky gray uniform of corporate monkeys. Driven red grouse in Scotland costs £50 a brace (two birds), and to make it worth the effort the minimum daily bag should never drop below 100 brace a day, for five days. Red-legged partridge in Spain run $50 a bird, and a good day's shooting with a 12-gun line may produce 800 or more partridges. A three-day, one-wagon, four-shooter wild bobwhite quail hunt on one of the best Thomasville, Georgia, plantations, including lodging and pretty much anything else one's heart desires, goes for $18,000. I know of a 3,000-acre quail lease near Tallahassee that is being offered for forty dollars an acre for seven years (that price does not include the expense of burning, harrowing, mowing, planting, fertilizing, or any supplemental feeding). I also know of a turnkey 6,000-acre plantation with a fine old house, stables, dog kennels, outbuildings, and plenty of wild quail ready to be shot; the asking price is thirteen million dollars.

That, unfortunately, is what top-of-the-line hunting fetches these days, and with more people and less available land, it is hard to envision things getting better. To all but the most affluent, the numbers and the lifestyle requisite for this form of sport hunting are inconceivable, even grotesque. Individuality, resolve, and improvisation are not part of the scenario. This is about guides, well-defined time slots, rules of etiquette, and pampering, lots of pampering. I was a shooter before I was a hunter and, being lazy as a cur, I understand the attraction of skies moved by ten thousand wings and I do enjoy feeling like a dandy in the whorehouse. The experience of that level of sport is memorable in every sense of the word, but I certainly understand how, to most hunters, spending that kind of money and displaying such a lack of exertion are at best farcical, at worst inequitable, and how poaching and revolutions evolved out of similar inequalities.

However, there is management at least, and management on a grand scale, without which game in the Southeast would be nonexistent. The habitat is, of course, being turned into cement. And two hundred and fifty million dollars a year worth of game is being poached—not to feed hungry families, not even by a bunch of knaves like myself who shoot an extra limit of doves once in a while to make up for leaner days, but poached for illegal sale to restaurants that cater to the affluent ninnies, to the Orientals with waning libidos, to those honchos who want their names in the record books but can't deal with the terrain, to the manufacturers of shoes and belts and women's coats, and on and on. Who is at fault: Me, you, the rich guy next door, evolution, God?

X

February 14, 1992

Winter was officially over for me today, Valentine's Day. The temperature shot up to 76, frogs sang, swallows swept over the pond above the reflection of the first cumulus clouds of the year activated by the sudden ground heat. Small flocks of bufflehead, lesser scaup, and ringnecks have joined the resident wood duck, mingling and feeding on the corn scattered in the shallows. The pond is fulfilling its role as a roadside inn on a long voyage home. In the afternoon lightning ripped over the panhandle, visiting one cloud after the other, rarely reaching the ground but turning the landscape into a religious enactment; it had been six months since I'd seen anything like it. Later that night a second front, a cold one, moved south, pushing the cumulus clouds ahead of it and upsetting what had been a normal thunderstorm. Five inches of rain poured out of the systems, the worst of it at four in the morning.

At daybreak, high winds hugged the farm and the colors of night barely changed from black to gray. Hawks and buzzards scoured the wind, heads down, looking for a storm kill. A great pine leaned over like a sailboat and never regained its balance, exposing its roots and a great slab of bleeding earth, a wedge of red clay that from a distance looked thin as a skillet. Later, I walked through the woods and counted 140 uprooted trees, trees that had at one time or another pulled my eyes to the sky.

The sun burrowed through the clouds two days later, stretching forgotten reflections over the lapping surface of the pond. From a distance the rafted ducks looked like little old men. The clay was slick underfoot. The dam was dark green. "Black grass," Bill called it. He had fertilized the rye before the rain. Dozens of yellow-bellied turtles took refuge on the free-floating logs that had risen from the bottom. The small male turtles swam circles around the logs and in a post-storm titillation of tortoise nerve cells desperately tried to mount the females as they hoisted themselves out of the water. The purchase wasn't there, and they kept falling back into the rough water. The females stretched their long leather necks to the brightening sun.

This is the first serious rain we have had since the end of September, and I watch my pond swell into a different body of water, powerful because of the land it claims as it feeds on the runoff. The surface rises before my eyes and takes possession of the bowl we intended her to fill. The lake takes on the demeanor and abundance of a full-breasted woman. Four wild geese—two Canadas and two snows—plow out of the early-morning dew that clings to the window of my study. Not an exceptional sight in Texas but certainly one in Gadsden County, Florida. The big birds heel over, exposing their bellies before fading into the dreamy mystery that is fog. Soon a bald eagle begins working the pond, as does an osprey, four anhingas, and a pair of otters. The pond is fertile with storm-stirred life. "You must kill the otters," they say, "or you won't have any fish left."

The osprey looks cold diving feetfirst into the water and missing brim. It falls in three times, each time floating on the surface, its wings cupping, flailing the water, finally rising into the air. Gator bait. The bald eagle makes a clean, legs-extended pass and departs carrying a bass in its talons.

The anhingas offer their wings to the wind. "Snake birds," they tell me, "rake the scales off bass too big for them to catch. The bass die from the parasites. Better shoot them."

I say, "I can always buy fish, but where am I going to buy an otter, or a water bird that swims like a snake?"

XI

There is just enough rock and roll left in me to dance to the music that brings back the memories. I dance in the fields, where no one sees me except the sun, the trees, and my dogs, who get upset when I act crazy. When I urge them to dance with me and they jump up and down they are happy again.

I dreamed the other night that I was back in Europe standing in the gravel courtyard of my parents' home, talking with the gamekeeper who, when I was seven years old, taught me how to shoot a gun and skin a rabbit. As we talked, and for no apparent reason, he pulled a bottle of red wine from his game pouch, uncorked it, and poured us each a glass. While he poured the drinks, another friend I hadn't seen in thirty years joined us, and he in turn was joined by another, and a fourth, and so on until the courtyard was full of people, all men I had hunted with during my lifetime, some faces stretching the extremes of remembrance. The men were my age and older, and as we stood together in the courtyard of my youth they raised their glasses, and I realized they were toasting me, and I didn't know why. I looked at the blurred faces of these friends, each of whom I remembered as if it were yesterday, and while the dream continued I relived the hunts we had made, the wine we had tasted, the food we had shared, and the women we had courted. And still this assembly of old men said nothing, waiting in the courtyard of my castle with their glasses raised, and I knew that something had happened.

Superimposed on these faces a new scene took shape. I saw through my dream a great red stag, chased by a pack of hounds and horses, feral men and women dressed in blue velvet uniforms, and me running alongside the stag. I ran so well, so flawlessly, I became a brother to this stag. And when my brother had swum the rivers and run his fill of fields and woods and was dark with sweat, and while he held the hounds at bay, I watched the flat, broad blade of a man's lance touch his rib cage, and saw the terror and wonder in my brother's eyes, alive and beseeching for an instant after everything else about him was dead. I felt the same, terrible glaze fall over my eyes, scalding my soul, and I knew someone had died, in the courtyard of my castle, and of course, it was me.

XII

A birder is a person who loves birds. Herbert L. Stoddard, ornithologist, naturalist, ecologist, and the most famous quail authority of the century, was known as a dreamer of birds; so was Aldo Leopold. These and many others loved and cared for birds passionately all their lives, and left behind the guidelines that we modest mortals have read, studied, and marveled at. Included in their reveries were the darker dreams of death and extinction that any caring lover broods about in the silence of darkness; in the case of bobwhite quail and a variety of other game birds, death would have included not only the birds necessary for their work, but birds shot from their own guns for pleasure. Stoddard and Leopold were bird hunters, and although they were hunters of a mindful kind, careful in the taking, thankful for the privilege of being alive and well in the woods at a time of year when the pursuit of game comes naturally, they nevertheless hunted with great enthusiasm and joy, pursuing a pastime they loved.

As a hunter I mourn the decline of habitat and the behavior of my peers; as a human being I mourn the poisoning of the earth; as a father I mourn the disappearance of so many feathered things; and as an ill-tempered recluse I mourn the passing of the pillory. Most of us have bowed our heads and offered our souls to a religion with a god; some of us have fought for causes that didn't include gods. Perhaps it's time to endorse a religion that has for a god a cause, such as saving what is left of what was here before we even believed in gods.

In a first time, I will hunt because I love to and I do it well; in a second time, I will do what all old men do: sit, drink, and reminisce on how it used to be; and finally I will pass on, leaving behind me the accretion of a few decades of a life, known in some circles as "a life of sport," useless in every respect. Insofar as the future of blood sports is concerned, I have this nagging feeling that killing for the motives I have killed for will seem as barbaric to the generations that follow as the behavior of market hunters and number hunters seems to me.

XIII

By winter, the roan-colored Brittany didn't look like a suckling pig anymore. He was thin and fit, the bones in his face had sharpened, his nose had swayed and lengthened, and his hindquarters had filled out. Carnac had graduated from looking like a pig to looking like a jackal, a twenty-four-pound jackal with a long nose, and at twenty-four pounds the perfect poacher's dog, built to jump into a game vest at the first sign of trouble. At one year old he was a "balls-to-the-wall" puppy who enjoyed life to its fullest, at the expense of everyone else, particularly the bitches. Knowing nothing about kennels, shock collars, or leather whips, Carnac has had no contact with the darker side of a hunting dog's life, so when I say "birds," stretching the *b*'s and the *r*'s, he looks at me, sits up straight as an arrow, and tests the air. His cheeks puff and unpuff, his nose inspecting the azimuth, and his eyes follow his nose. He is stationary hunting.

Carnac was a natural from his first day in the field. He loved the grass, the briars, the smells, and had been taught early that the sound of a gun is a moment to relish, beginning with the feral pigs that I sometimes shot in the ass with a .410 to move them out of the yard. Carnac hates pigs ever since the morning he and Robin ran out of the lake house into the legs of a sow and her four piglets rooting up the grass for worms. The sow cornered the Brittany against the side of the house and tried to eat him, scaring the stink out of both dogs—and me. I hit the pig over the head with a shovel, hard, until she finally turned on me, allowing the dogs to get away before rendering any meat, but it was close. Carnac does not have a problem with guns.

He pointed a quail wing within a minute of watching it fly at the end of a fishing pole, but that doesn't mean too much. A trainer once bragged, "Hell, I can get my wife to point if she wants something bad enough." I bought some pen-raised quail, built a call-back pen, and began training the puppy. The only thing that didn't work was that the quail that were supposed to return to their plywood home before dark never did, choosing instead to join the wild ones. Can't say I blame them.

Carnac learned how to run through a field chasing birds that smelled good, and one day, just like my trainer friend told me he would, the puppy realized he couldn't catch them and pointed. Pointed, solid as Excalibur.

A week after that the dog pulled a check cord

through the woods and learned to whoa, which he did only to please me. By late summer he began finding a few wild coveys and learned about the sound of a dozen wings. Carnac began to follow his long shovel nose, which rarely deceived him. If he smelled birds, he trailed them until he found them. The dog is stubborn.

Meanwhile, my doltish pointer, Mabel, managed to fall asleep under a truck and, oblivious to the engine noise, allowed herself to be run over, dislocating her hip. Once it was mended she did what she had always hoped for: she never left her chair. So much for her vacuous career. Mabel has since moved in with a lady who doesn't hunt but enjoys dressing her in Victorian clothes. The age of the big-going dogs is over for me. Now I sneak around with a tiny dog that walks on its hind legs to see over cover, cocks one of them to take a piss, and looks goofy when the smell of feathers passes his way.

I introduced a blank pistol into the picture a few weeks into fall and the dog is now convinced that life is one big bowl of food, boners, and birds. When the sounds of wings and gunfire became inseparable entities in Carnac's mind and I was able to hold him on point through the flush without raising my voice, I started calling up friends, praising the poacher dog's abilities. I lied a little too, just to make sure they knew what a fine animal had graced my jubilee year, the dog that will hunt me to my sixties.

At home, Carnac missed few opportunities to display the flip side of his character. He kept right on eating rugs, shoes, the springer's tail, and, whenever the opportunity presented itself, he wrapped his front legs around anything that felt right and humped it until his eyes glazed with happiness. Carnac is not popular with those who don't know or care about his split personality. He is with me.

Graduation day came on an overcast winter morning, full of fog and pale shadows. I released him into a section of the farm where I had heard quail whistling and watched proudly as the little dog cast back and forth, looking at me for direction, moving with a special eagerness, as if his instincts were telling him that this was what all those weeks of training had been about. The terrain sloped through a mixed cover of grass, year-old oak saplings, and myrtle bushes to a small corn-field cut into an open bench in the middle of the woods. Half the corn was standing. The rest had been mowed down. There was grain on the ground. The deer had taken to the field, as had the turkeys and at least two coveys of bobwhite quail. The wind was right, it was early in the day, and wild smells sprang out of the dew.

Carnac worked on fifty yards ahead of me, looking pretty sure of himself. Quail had always been easy for him to find before, and he saw no reason why they wouldn't be on this day.

When he stopped, he had a face full of bird scent and, except for a speeding tail and puffing cheeks, he stared ahead and didn't move. The scene warmed the cockles of my heart. This was the first of our salad days together. I walked up be-hind the dog, quietly reminding him to stay, walked to a piece of low cover, and watched a good covey of bobwhite quail hurl itself off the ground and fan over the cornfield. No doubles today, I thought, and, assuring the shot, dropped a bird twenty-five yards away.

"All right, little man," I said, "fetch it up." I was feeling pretty good about the developments.

The Brittany broke for the bird while I reloaded and thought about having a glass of wine for lunch, a big one, to mark the occasion and adjust my personality. Carnac ran behind a stand of tall dog fennel. I must have crippled that bird, I thought heading his way; what a good dog I have. I encouraged him from the far side of the fennel stand, and when I got around to where I could see, there he was, facing away from me, muzzle in a bush, tail wagging. It looked to me that he had the bird, so I told him to fetch it back. He didn't, so I told him to sit, which he did in his ramrod fashion. No problem, I thought; he pointed, held, and then found the bird. I didn't expect as much on his first day out—after all, perfection is elusive. I broke the gun, walked up behind the puppy, and reached around his head for the quail in his mouth. The only thing my fingers encountered were two scaly feet, which when pulled on surrendered, and came free.

The rest of the bird shot straight down Carnac's throat.

Bibliography

Bell, C. Ritchie, and Bryan J. Taylor. *Florida Wild Flowers and Road-side Plants*. Chapel Hill: Laurel Hill Press, 1982.

Bradley, A. G. *Sketches from Old Virginia*. London: Macmillan and Co., 1897.

Cleveland, Clover. *Fishing and Shooting Sketches*. New York: The Outing Publishing Co., 1907.

Courtine, Robert J., ed. *Larousse Gastronomique*. Paris, France: Larousse, 1938.

Eiseley, Loren. *The Star Thrower*. New York: Harcourt Brace Jovanovich, 1978.

Gringoire, Th., and L. Saulnier. *Le Répertoire de la Cuisine*. Paris, France: Dupont et Malgat-Guériny.

Hudson, Charles. *The Southeastern Indians*. Knoxville: The University of Tennessee Press, 1976.

Krider's Sporting Anecdotes. New York: Abercrombie & Fitch Co., 1966.

Landers, J. Larry, and Brad S. Mueller. *Bobwhite Quail Management: A Habitat Approach*. Tallahassee: Tall Timbers Research Station, 1986.

Lanier, Henry Wysham. *The Land of Bob White*. Washington, D.C.: Southern Railway System, 1923.

Lewis, Elisha, J., M.D. *The American Sportsman*. Philadelphia and London: J. B. Lippincott Co., 1906.

McFarland, David, ed. *The Oxford Companion to Animal Behavior*. London: Oxford University Press, 1987.

Ripley, Ozark. *Quail and the Quail Dog*. Columbus, Ohio: The Hunter-Trader-Trapper Co., 1939.

Rosene, Walter, and John D. Freeman. *A Guide to and Culture of Flowering Plants and Their Seed Important to Bobwhite Quail*. Augusta, GA: Morris Communication Corporation, 1988.

Stoddard, Herbert L. *The Bobwhite Quail: Its Habits, Preservation and Increase*. New York: Charles Scribners, 1950.

————. *Memoirs of a Naturalist*. Norman: University of Oklahoma Press, 1969.

Venters, Vic. "Breakthrough on Bobwhites?" *Quail Unlimited*, July–August 1992.

Willoughby, Francis. *The Ornithology*. Printed by A.C. for John Martyn, Printers to the Royal Society, at the Bell in St. Paul's Church-Yard, London, 1678.

Wilson, Edward O. *Biophilia*. Cambridge, MA: Harvard University Press, 1984.